FROM TIME TO ETERNITY

From Time to Eternity

ESSAYS ON DANTE'S *DIVINE COMEDY*

Edited by Thomas G. Bergin

Yale University Press
New Haven and London
1967

Preface

The six essays that compose this book were delivered under the auspices of the Division of Humanities of Yale University, October 1965, in commemoration of the 700th anniversary of Dante's birth.

Although the lecturers were given complete freedom in their choice of subject, the topics treated do form a book in which one chapter leads very naturally into another. Professor Sapegno's lecture discusses the general problem of the genesis of the *Comedy,* both as a product of its times and as a manifestation of the inner crisis of the poet. Professor Morghen explores in depth the Florentine scene which has such a large part in this genesis—at least in its first aspect, and Professor Petrocchi discusses the intellectual currents of the times, particularly as affecting the ethical and religious attitudes developed in the *Comedy.* Father Foster and Professor Greene are concerned with two general themes that run through the poem, and Professor Scaglione offers a consideration of the poet's technique in an area in which his art has been especially admired. Thus the lectures proceed from a survey of sources, or one might say raw materials, to an analysis of the fin-

PREFACE

ished product, from a study of some of the dominant motifs of the poem to comment on its mechanics, or lastly, in the poet's own words, "e di Fiorenza in popol giusto e sano." Very appropriately the central chapters deal with Dante's study and exposition of divine love, that force which "moves the sun and the other stars" and is the deepest source of the poet's inspiration.

It was my happy privilege to organize the series of lectures and to prepare this manuscript for publication. If I may do so without presumption I should like to express my thanks to the lecturers for their participation in the enterprise. I should also like to thank the Provost of the University for his help in finding funds to defray expenses for the series, the Secretary for his cooperation in making the endowments of the Woodward and Trumbull Lectureships available and the Amity Club of New Haven for its generous contribution to the undertaking. I am personally very grateful to Professor Franco Simone and Miss Mary Ann Rizzo for special aid, cheerfully volunteered.

Thomas G. Bergin

A Note on Translations

The lectures of Professors Sapegno, Morghen, and Petrocchi were given in Italian and have been translated by Mary Ann Rizzo. For the English version of quotations from the *Divine Comedy,* Miss Rizzo has used the translation of H. R. Huse, New York–Toronto, 1954, save for a few brief phrases where she has translated directly. The sources of the English version of other works of Dante are indicated on the appropriate pages. Father Foster and Professors Greene and Scaglione, whose lectures were delivered in English, have indicated the source of their quotations wherever they used translations other than their own.

All the quotations from Dante's works are from *Le opere di Dante* (2d ed., Florence, Società dantesca italiana, 1960).

Contents

I.

How the Commedia *Was Born*

BY NATALINO SAPEGNO

Professor of Italian Literature,
University of Rome

The topic I wish to discuss—"How the *Commedia*
Was Born" (Come nasce la *Commedia*)—can be ap-
proached in two ways. The first is external, by tracing
the spatial and temporal coordinates in the composition of the *Commedia* (or, as Dante probably pronounced it, *Comedía*), thus establishing how, when,
and where Dante composed this work. The second can
be done internally, by attempting to see from within
how, under the biographical and historical conditions
of a particular moment in Italian and European civilization, a concept such as the Dantesque poem, so vast
in foundation and grandiose in size, could have taken
shape.

The external problem can be quickly resolved for
the data we possess are so scarce that we can actually
say very little about the exact conditions of time and
place in which the poem was conceived. However, this
little is at least sufficient to establish, if nothing else,

a basis that I believe essential to a more profound and internal definition of the theme we have proposed. Certain references we possess—and the only reliable ones—state that the first two parts of the *Commedia* had already been circulated and were known in 1313. Other references indicate that the last part, the *Paradiso,* was composed in the last years of Dante's life, between 1316 and 1321, and that Dante had barely finished its composition at the time of his death. Another established fact is that the writing of the *Commedia* spanned almost the entire second period of Dante's life, that period beginning with his exile. We are not dealing with a rapidly composed work, but with one written slowly and one which, notwithstanding the fundamental unity of its conception, reflects the changes and transformations taking place in Dante's mind throughout that time.

Coming now to what I consider most important, the internal problem, the task is to explain what might be called the genesis of the *Commedia*—the biographical and historical genesis of a work deeply rooted in a determinate moment of human civilization. Clearly, we must begin with certain facts of Dante's life, above all, its crucial and fundamental moment, his exile. It has been said many times that without the exile a work such as the *Commedia* would perhaps never have been born. Without the exile, there would never have fused in Dante certain conditions, certain sentimental and intellectual reactions, giving rise to the idea of such a work.

This exile represents a deep crisis, one that has certain elements of remote preparation even in the preceding phase of Dante's life and one that ultimately affects all aspects of it. His religious conviction, political theory, mental state, and philosophical preparation all converge in that moment of exile in which Dante awakens not merely to an abstract, theoretical realization or consciousness, but to a personal consciousness, one paid for with his own existence and therefore deeply felt. He takes cognizance of the profound crisis investing all aspects of European and Christian civilization—a waning medieval civilization.

Dante lived in an era that saw the end of a long, secular tradition of a civilization which had been modified through time but nevertheless had preserved a basic compactness. Dante perfected a consciousness of this crisis through his own situation—as a man who had entered the political scene of his commune and had been overthrown by this political struggle; as a man who had seen the forms of his previous existence destroyed and who had been obliged to abandon home, wife, and children—everything he most dearly cherished.

It is at this point that Dante becomes aware of the intense change taking place around him, and he studies its causes. He strives to fit those components of his personal crisis into the framework of a vision that rationally and systematically contemplates all aspects of existence, all manifestations of civilization. It is then that Dante passes a severe judgment on his contemporary society, arising from his awareness of that profound crisis undermining contemporary civilization. This is the waning of the Middle Ages, with all aspects of medieval life decaying while Dante—the man who is to be the last great poet and interpreter of medieval civilization—is still alive, a witness to this degeneration, this disintegration. But he will defend them to the end and cling to them as a last resource of possible salvation—the only path he can see.

This all-encompassing intellectual and social upheaval can also be examined objectively, independently of the verdict Dante gives us, for it is his merit to have had full cognizance of the crisis, having made himself its interpreter, having searched for its solution, but above all having sought to place it beyond his own subjective level. The latter is a constant characteristic of all his works and activities, beginning with the *Vita Nuova* in which he transformed a youthful love experience into an objective problem of universal character, intent upon formulating a casuistry going well beyond his personal case.

We can examine objectively the downfall of the universal forms—the Church and the Empire, the highest regulator of spiritual and religious life on the one hand, and of political and social life on the other —a collapse universally recognized and therefore destructive to the prestige of these bodies. This occurs during the same years in Dante's life that witness a last futile attempt at imperial restoration in Italy by Henry VII and that see in the slap at Anagni the decline of the Papacy and its subsequent subservience to the House of France. An abysmal decadence is felt in the institutions peculiar to Italian civilization—for example, the communes which, just at that time, were beginning to reveal their inability to transcend certain limits of essentially corporative politics. The communes were incapable of assimilating the forces from the rural areas which were brutally subdued and enslaved, as likewise the lesser communes were subjugated by the greater ones.

Decadence was attacking not only these aspects of the political scene, but moral and intellectual life as well. Dante continually emphasizes this situation in his work—the degeneration of personal behavior and municipal traditions; above all, the breakdown of those customs prevailing among the various factions that were becoming evermore terrible, ruthless, and pitiless. The deterioration was reaching beyond this level to an even more important one. Spirituality and religious life became corrupt; perverted by new ambitions for wealth and power, they lost strength and direction and abandoned their primary function, their mission. There was deterioration in the field of science and in intellectual life because the cohesion, structure, and compactness of Scholastic thought had begun to weaken. It must be remembered that this was occurring during the life of the poet generally considered a representative—indeed, almost a parallel manifestation—of Scholasticism and, in particular, of Thomism. The firm belief in the possibility of reconciling reason and faith, revelation and science, Aristotelianism and the Scriptures—the deep faith that had been so keen and firm in St. Thomas' Scholasticism—weakened at the end of the thirteenth and the beginning of the fourteenth centuries with the rise of speculative currents in the very bosom of Scholasticism. These currents reverted to fideistic positions denying the possibility of agreement between reason and faith and tending to assert faith, revelation, and the Scriptures above and beyond the field of reason.

We have spoken of decadence because we have been looking at the era through Dante's eyes. In truth, this "decadence" marks a radical transformation which, through the crisis of universal authorities, had already brought about the creation in the political field of private nations and private states or, at any rate, private states in Italy—for example, the "Signorie" and the "Principati." In the realm of thought, it was effecting a profound change, passing from the rationalistic conceptions of Aristotelian Scholasticism to the very different ones that would carry through to the development of Humanism. One has only to think of the attitude of the men belonging to the generation immediately succeeding Dante's. Petrarch or Boccaccio already operated in a world of thought which no longer admitted the possibility of a system or of intellectual order, where intellectual activity itself tended to operate within an ever-narrowing field. The figure of man —the individual—was enclosed within the landscape and refused to be concerned with the problems of the cosmos, the totality of the universe.

As I have already stated, this transformation presented itself to Dante as decadence, as the abandonment of certain positions in which man felt supported, guided, protected—and set within the bounds of a precise design, clear, firm, and rigid—and from which he was emerging to find himself in a sort of chaos, an intellectual and social anarchy.

Dante's whole poem makes vivid this predicament. The pages of the *Commedia* that can be cited to char-

6

acterize and define this scene of deterioration are infinite. From these pages emerges a deeply pessimistic view of mankind's state at that time. This pessimism is born in the poet's soul after his exile; it is evident in his works written at this time, in which there is a growing sense of solitude and isolation from a world he no longer understands or, at least, refuses to understand or accept.

We begin to notice this attitude in poems that are perhaps anterior to the conception of the *Commedia* or written in the days when Dante first started thinking of the poem. From its inception, this attitude carries with it a sense of pride—pride for its own solitude, and the pride of a man who considers himself as having remained faithful to a dying way of life; he *alone* faithful, he *alone* still capable of upholding concepts and institutions of valor and virtue, the guide words of medieval Christian civilization.

Think of that canzone in which Dante envisions justice and the other virtues as degraded, abandoned, rejected, disparaged by men. In contrast to this attitude, he feels the merit of his own solitude. In face of the fact that virtue is rejected by the world, shunned by mankind while vice triumphs, Dante, siding with virtue, feels proud to be like the latter. He will say, "The exile I have been given, I count an honor" (L'esilio che m'è dato, onor mi tegno). This exile is an honor for me if I share it with the virtues, the highest values of human life, which men are no longer capable of understanding and which they now disparage.

There is another poem that brings to the surface the fundamental concept that Dante will oppose to this

7

condition of decadence. It is a sonnet written to invoke God's intervention in raising up again the lot of justice on earth—justice that has been abandoned, scorned, and denied by all. He asks God, "This virtue which lies nude and cold/raise her up, clothed by Your veil/ for without her there is no peace here on earth" (Questa virtù che nuda e fredda giace/levala su, vestita del tuo velo/che sanza lei non è in terra pace). There is already in these verses the essential nucleus of the concept Dante will oppose to the decay, disorder, and anarchy of his time.

Justice is fallen today, but God can make it rise up once more. Only justice is the guarantor of humanity's fate. Justice alone can ensure the progress and continuity of human civilization, for without it there is no peace on earth. Justice is the foundation of peace. From this primitive nucleus, we know that Dante developed these ideas throughout his works, commencing with the last book of the *Convivio* and ending with the *Monarchia,* the treatise in which he most systematically advanced his opinions. He may have written the latter during the years of Henry VII's decline or, as seems more probable nowadays, in the very last years of his life, thinking of it as his last message to the world, to distorted mankind. All of its pages center about the necessity of reestablishing justice, the principles of order, peace, and even liberty. For disorder arises precisely from the failure of what had been the connective elements that made something orderly out of the concept of life in all its aspects; a collective conviction based on forces capable of putting order in the universe—a mental universe as well as man's civil universe. This order can only be assured by an agent that will eliminate the essential principle of discord which, as Dante sets forth in a famous page of the *Convivio,* is greed, that is to say, the desire to increase one's own might, wealth, and power. This unrestrainable greed which is at the bottom of corrupt human nature is the cause of social discord and wars between kingdoms. Such wars in turn are responsible for strife between cities and within cities; their tribulations are felt in the city wards and down to the individual homes. Thus mankind's hope of happiness is everywhere frustrated.

In other words, all human conflicts originate in greed. These conflicts begin between kingdoms but end by sinking their roots down into the conscience of the individual since, through the various hierarchies in which man is ordered on earth, those that Dante calls cities, neighborhoods, and homes, strife comes to lacerate and destroy the respect for order in the conscience of the individual.

This state of anarchy and disorder can be changed only by the presence of a force or authority above every private or sectarian power "that possessing all, he may not have further desire to possess anything" (tutto possedendo e più desiderare non possendo). As we know, Dante identified this force with the Emperor. This doctrine might seem to us remote and antiquated, but I believe there is something in its core that can still be important.

In any case, for Dante it was a question of reconstituting a form of reality, a way of life, that would restore what was becoming impossible in the present state of affairs. We have read Dante's words, "happiness is rendered impossible in this manner" (così si impedisce la felicitade). Man can no longer be happy, and we must therefore be concerned with rebuilding a world in which he can regain happiness.

When Dante, in one of his later epistles—the letter to Can Grande della Scala—explains his objectives in composing the *Commedia,* he expresses himself in this way: It is a question, he says, of removing man "from the condition of misery" (de statu miserie) and unhappiness in which he finds himself "and leading him back to a condition of happiness" (et reducere eum ad statum felicitatis). This was the purpose Dante explicitly had in mind in writing his poem. The notion of this purpose arose precisely from Dante's deep awareness of the personal crisis through which he was passing and the cultural crisis in which he was living.

In the *Commedia* we can trace the threads of the diagnosis Dante makes of the condition of society in his day. We begin with those episodes in which he examines the ruthless ferocity of the struggles waged by the factions within the commune—the decadence he warned against was already deep-rooted in the present state of Florence. He placed the blame on the advent of newcomers, quick profits, the nouveaux riches, and those obsessed by the dream of wealth. We note next the episodes in which his glance extends over conditions prevailing throughout all Italy, with the equally ferocious and ruthless quarrels between the various Italian states. Finally, as yet other episodes in the *Commedia* reveal, he expands his outlook to contemplate the conditions of all Christian and European society and to alert all realms—though his knowledge of the actual situation in these kingdoms, particularly the distant ones, must have been scanty and vague—to the progress of decadence by which today's sovereigns are certainly worse than yesterday's, and tomorrow's will be worse yet.

If we pass on to those other episodes where Dante sinks his knife still deeper into the flesh of contemporary society, we come to those pages dedicated to describing in various ways what Dante considers the nucleus of this general corruption. This nucleus is the failure and corruption of religion, spirituality—the failure of the Church herself in fulfilling her mission. These are the famous pages of terrible invective against the men of the Church, the pages in which Dante examines the abysmal downfall of the once-great religious and monastic institutions that had had so profound and vast a function in medieval life. They are the pages on St. Benedict, Peter Damian, St. Francis, and St. Dominic.

There are passages, too, where Dante considers the decline of sincere interest in speculation, now subordinated to the pursuit of the practical and materialistic even in the intellectual sphere. Dante accuses the clerics themselves of abandoning St. Augustine, St. Ambrose, and Gregory the Great, because all their attention has been turned instead to studying the decretals—that is to say, the things that could furnish them with riches, prebends, privileges, etc.

It is a profoundly bitter presentation which springs from thousands of episodes in the *Commedia* and is, we might say, at the very root of the *Commedia's* conception. In Dante's words, therefore, this conception proposed to restore mankind to the state of happiness. This could come about only through God's direct intervention because the world seemed to be headed toward a chasm, toward growing anarchy and ruin.

There is a letter—perhaps Dante's most beautiful letter—written to the Italian cardinals meeting at the conclave in Carpentras to elect a new pope after the death of Clement V. From this letter emerges Dante's vision of decay and disorder sapping the fundamental forces, the most vital elements of the intellectual and moral life of the times. In opposition to these things, Dante rises in solitude—he who is not a cleric, he who bears no authority and has no privilege to support his words. He alone rises to point out the growing evil and to ask for God's vengeance and intercession, while at the same time asking men themselves to cooperate in the work of renewal and redemption. The wording used by Dante in this letter which is replete with biblical phrases is quite touching: "Of the sheep in Christ's flock, I am one of the least, for I am not wealthy. Not through riches, but by Grace of God I am what I am, and the zeal for God's house consumes me" (Fra le pecorelle della gregge di Cristo, io sono una delle minime chè non ho ricchezze. Non per forza di ricchezze ma per la grazia di Dio io sono ciò che sono, e lo zelo della casa di Dio mi consuma. *Quippe de ovibus pascuis Iesu Christi minima una sum . . . quoniam divitiae mecum non sunt. Non ergo divitiarum, sed gratia Dei sum id quod sum, et zelus domus eius me comedit*'). Not without God's will and inspiration does it happen that of the great number who usurp the office of shepherd (pastor), the solitary pious voice among so many sheep, if not exactly unattended, certainly neglected and unprotected in the pastures, is that of a private citizen. "One voice alone—alone piteous and only a private one—is heard at the obsequies, as it were, of Mother Church" (Una sola vox, sola pia, et hec privata, in matris Ecclesie quasi funere audiatur). The funeral of Mother Church is, for Dante, the funeral of all Christianity.

The corruption that has invaded spirituality and religion has extended to all fields. This has happened precisely because the Church has forgotten her function, her religious mission, in order to turn to illusions of power and wealth and to interfere in fields of activity not properly hers. It is for this reason the world is in disorder and the imperial authority is no longer recognized. Because of this, justice has failed and peace and liberty no longer exist for man. For without this divinely ordained order constituted in the two forms that are imperial authority (the supreme arbiter above all individual and local sovereignties) and religious force (represented by the Church), mankind cannot be truly guided to happiness on earth or to bliss in the life to come.

Dante feels himself invested with this mission and thus authorized to speak as a prophet and to address other men as a prophet. This is the moment, the historical and biographical moment, in which Dante elaborates the conception of his poem and does so in that particular form; he elaborates the grandiose concept that his poem must be a warning to all humanity to set it once more on the straight path. For Dante it is a return to the past. It is not an acceptance of the crisis but rather a clinging to those values which the new society has forgotten and destroyed.

While he works out this theme of a prophecy to renew a systematic and organic vision of the world, he also elaborates on the instrument of this poetry—its form, that is, what we call the invention of the other world, the voyage into the beyond. This idea is a striking device that allows Dante to shape the essential purpose of his invention, which is to express his judgment on the reality of his times. It permits him to create a grand perspective through which all of present reality—the world of daily events, the ephemeral and contingent world—comes to be examined, evaluated, and judged in comparison with the eternal, immobile, and perfect world. It is precisely this possibility of a twofold vision, the comparison continually drawn between fleeting reality, earthly chaos, and the order constituted by God, which permits Dante to base his severe judgment on a secure platform of authority.

It is clear that Dante's position, his starting point, contains a fundamental dichotomy. On the one hand, there is an attitude of antithesis and rejection regarding the world he sees in decay, cast into disorder and chaos, be it from the viewpoint of doctrines or from the viewpoint of institutions. On the other hand, there is an attitude of intense participation because Dante clearly does not base his rejection on disinterest or indifference. His rejection is passionate and engagé; there is always implicit in it the desire for renewal, the quest for some way of changing the pattern of decadence.

The effect of this dichotomy in the composition of the poem is to create a persistent tension; it is responsible for what might be called the intensely dramatic character of the Dantesque representation. It also carries with it a change in the Dantesque attitude through time. If we wished to draw up a kind of chart of the diverse evolution of these two attitudes of rejection and participation, we could say that the sense of participation and commitment, the outspoken invectives against the reality of his time, while strongest at the beginning and constituting the first stimulus and basis from which the inspiration arose, becomes gradually mitigated. In the last *cantica,* it gives place to an attitude not of indifference but of authoritative detachment, in virtue of which the invectives of the *Paradiso* (for we find them there, too) have a different accent. They are voiced by saints and therefore are characterized by a tone of authority, severity, and remoteness. They no longer have the violence and impetus of the invectives in the *Inferno,* where Dante comes to confuse the reality of Infernal life with the reality he was witnessing around him on earth. In the framework of the passions and Infernal disorder, Dante saw mirrored exactly the confusion and anarchy of the contemporary conditions in Italy and Europe.

While this element of participation diminishes with the passing years, though does not disappear entirely, Dante's attitude of rejection and antithesis operates in inverse order. Initially less marked, it gains strength as Dante's polemic attitude of immediate participation gradually weakens. It is therefore in the *Paradiso* that we see this refusal assume its most precise and marked form—that of detachment from the ephemeral world —explicit in the comparison he draws between what he calls the "examples" (l'esemplo) and the "exemplary" (l'esemplare), that is, the things of the earthly world and the divine examples, the divine ideas upon which human reality models itself. With this growing detachment come the pages in the *Paradiso* where Dante contemplates from on high this little globe, this wretched earth that is a nothingness compared to celestial reality and yet is so bloodied by human strife, "the threshing floor that makes us so ruthless" (l'aiuola che ci fa tanto feroci).

This is the attitude we have sought in Dante and which we have tried to illustrate. From this nucleus, from this root was born the inspiration of the *Commedia*. It was born with those characteristics familiar to all of us—with that violence, with that impetus which characterized it from its inception, with that force of passion with which Dante invested his world—his next world—with a graphic and persuasive realism.

The *Commedia* originates, therefore, as a work embodying the extreme expression of medieval civilization and culture. It is the work of a man still accepting the mentality, order, structure, and institutions of the Middle Ages. In fact, Dante clings more tenaciously to them the more he sees them dissipated and dissolved around him.

This is Dante, the medieval man. This is the Dante who seems to look only to the past, the Dante who, to the men immediately following him—the men of the fourteenth century—already seems far-off, because they are living in a greatly changed era. Dante's pessimistic vision—one we might call conservative—is a vision that the men of the nascent humanistic period

are no longer capable of appreciating and understanding.

A problem arises here, one which is in fact extraneous to the topic I have undertaken but which emerges
almost spontaneously from the way in which I have
stated my theme. How can a poet who seems totally
immersed in the past, whose masterpiece springs from
a rejection of all those things that were the embryonic
forms of humanism and the Renaissance, who seems
so remote from us in concepts, ideals, and sentiments
still be a living force? How is it that he can still reach
us, still express something that impresses our minds
and hearts, still touch and stir our imagination?

Now of course, this is due first of all to Dante's
power of suggestion, to the fact that this re-creation
and reconstruction of a world in dissolution was not
set forth in the form of a doctrinal treatise but rather
in the form of a poem. It is a poem with an extraordinary wealth of invention; with the creation of a whole
landscape, an entire world; with an infinite series of
characters; with a plot intricately woven and rich in
images; with a language that is still alive in Italy today.

This poetic vigor is the essential source of the vitality
of the poet's work. But this I think is not the whole
answer, for the problem is somewhat more compli-
cated. That is to say, Dante's message does not live
solely as a poetic message, or, to state it better, it is
impossible to separate the imaginative, the poetic element in this message from its substance, the content
of sentiments and thoughts that give it life.

It happened to Dante as to other men in periods of
profound crisis and transformations in society; in

periods during which all the values created by the preceding centuries seem to be destroyed; when in the effort to adopt new positions and invent new themes, the vital and positive elements of the past are discarded. As it may have happened to Erasmus or to Thomas More in the stands they took during the Reformation, so it befell Dante to be the representative of those attempting to sustain the values of past civilization. These are the values which deserve to be saved as a heritage, to which mankind will return after the moment of crisis, the moment of the rupture that is necessarily a time of laceration and destruction. Certain values that are at the root of the inspiration of Dante's work—that quest for justice restored to its spiritual realm; that duty of rejection of divisive forces in the name of an idea transcending and regulating them; that necessity of a supreme arbitrator terminating the strife brought on by greed and reestablishing peace among men—these are values to which even today's men can profitably return in their meditation.

I would even say that these are values which today's civilization is slowly beginning to recover after centuries of violent outbursts of strife and destruction. In this sense, we hope that the Dantesque message will continue to speak as it has spoken—and our meeting today demonstrates this fact to men throughout the world—and we hope that the word of Dante will continue to be what he wanted it to be, something more than a pure poetic message, not merely a beautiful word but a persuasive and living word.

2.

Dante and the Florence of the Good Old Days

BY RAFFAELLO MORGHEN
Professor of Medieval History,
University of Rome

In Cantos XV and XVI of the *Paradiso,* which are devoted to the meeting of Dante with his ancestor Cacciaguida in the heaven of Mars, the *Commedia* finds its central point and complete justification. In these cantos, the poet's solemn affirmation of his civil and religious mission fuses with the most significant expression of the poetic and moral content of the poem. Autobiographical and universal elements combine, emphasized by the comparison of present corruption and the pure untainted past. This moment reflects both the vision of reality of the last medieval man and the anticipation of the first modern man, looking toward the future and aware of human dignity, glory, love, reason, and art.

Ideally connected with these cantos are those that we might call autobiographical, containing the prophecies of Ciacco, Ser Brunetto, Farinata, Vanni Fucci, and Forese Donati and full of nostalgic remembrance of the good old days when honor and courtesy (onore e cortesia) reigned in the world. Of like substance are those cantos of the *Paradiso* in which the degeneration of the religious orders and the Church is deplored by St. Benedict, St. Thomas, St. Bonaventure, and St. Peter in passages of vehement denunciations. Thus, actual experience and tradition, political passion and spiritual ideals, human love and hatred all come together in that representation of the society in which the poet lived and which he, by the concreteness with which he had portrayed it, knew how to transfigure into a moral world of exemplary universality.

Dante was born about the mid-thirteenth century, exactly five years after the fateful 1260, the year of the flagellant movement and the spasmodic expectation of the end of the world.[1] Since the beginning of the thirteenth century, Gioachino da Fiore had given a new impulse to the eschatological myth, looking to the forthcoming inauguration of the "Reign of the Spirit" (Regno dello Spirito) and expressing the longing for renewal and redemption that had influenced the whole century. Into this time of spiritual vigil, of expectation of events destined to resolve the contradictions of a civilization which had already exhausted all its strength in its creative effort, the Dantesque vision entered—a vision born not so much from a literary intent as from an authentic experience of action and thought, illuminated in a moment of grace, in the consciousness of a

1. R. Morghen, "Ranieri Fasani e il movimento dei Disciplinati del 1260," in *Il movimento dei Disciplinati nel Settimo Centenario dal suo inizio,* Atti del Convegno Internazionale, Perugia, Sept. 25–28, 1960 (Perugia, 1962).

moral and religious mission entrusted to the poet from Above. If one recalls that the eschatological vigil, the eager expectation of great and definitive events fated to close in a single moment of history the complete record of mankind on earth, recurs continually in the tradition of medieval Christianity, and that such an expectation reached tones of exasperated dramatic power in the "gioachimisimo" of the thirteenth century;[2] if one recalls the forecasts of Fra Salimbene or Fra Dolcino, which were Joachimite in tone, not to mention the supernatural mission of restorer of Rome, the Empire, and the Church claimed by Cola da Rienzo, Knight of the Holy Spirit, after Dante had been dead more than twenty years—then the profoundly eschatological inspiration from which the vision of the Dantesque poem also sprang will not seem difficult to understand.

As early as the tenth century Oddone di Cluny, in his *Occupatio,* had evoked anew in a didactic poem, in harsh verses and with involute ideas, the history of mankind from Adam down to the spreading corruption of his own times in order to induce his contemporaries to repentance in the imminence of God's judgment.[3] Dante, though with the quite different felicity of a poet, was moved by the same inspiration. However, the earthly world that in Oddone tended to

2. See the Atti del III Convegno Storico Internazionale called by the Accademia Tudertina on the topic *L'attesa dell'etá nuova nella spiritualitá della fine del Medioevo,* Todi, Oct. 16–19, 1960 (Todi, 1962).

3. R. Morghen, "Riforma monastica e spiritualitá cluniacense," from the Atti del Convegno Storico Internazionale on the topic of *Spiritualitá cluniacense* (Todi, 1960).

vanish from view in the routine deprecations of monastic asceticism assumed in Dante new dimensions and a new validity. It carried into the beyond the passions and ideals of human life, often placing them in the foreground, even in the presence of the luminous refulgence of eternal hope.

That is why in Dante's work the description of the society of the time appears in the immediateness of moral judgment with a vivacity that makes it one of the most significant documents of the social life of the latter Middle Ages, while the eschatological vision which influenced it gave to that representation a validity consonant with the civil and religious ideals of the poet. It was a moral judgment mainly unfavorable, in the name of God's law, meant to establish with a verdict unappealable in the beyond the equilibrium between free will and divine justice that had been broken by human passions and wickedness. It is evident that contemporary society appeared to Dante corrupt and evil because of the failure of the two suns that, in the words of Mark the Lombard, the wise man of government in the generation preceding Dante's, should "point out both paths, that of the world and that of God" (far vedere agli uomini l'una e l'altra strada e del mondo e di Dio—*Purgatorio* XVI).[4] Thus it is a twofold road that, on the one hand, in accordance with the word of God and the leadership of the Pontiff, should have led mankind to eternal happiness and, on the other hand, should have brought it to earthly hap-

4. Since the entire canto is devoted to Mark the Lombard it is superfluous to cite single verses.

piness through the faculty of reason and under the guidance of the Empire.

For Dante, therefore, the contemporary world—that world of politics, of men of arms and government, of poets, of epicureans whom he knew through direct and personal experience—was "devoid of every virtue" (diserto d'ogni virtute) since the "sword was joined with the shepherd's crook" (la spada è giunta col pastorale). It was a world that ensnared him with its sufferings and troubles at a time when he was participating in the fashionable round of gay parties or contending in rhymes with Forese Donati or Cecco Angiolieri, when he was engaged in not altogether platonic love affairs or occupying positions of prominence and responsibility in the convulsive political life of the times. This was the world of Brunetto Latini, the unforgettable teacher of humanity; of Tegghiaio Aldobrandini degli Adimari and Jacopo Rusticucci, who "set their minds to doing good" (a ben fare puoser gl'ingegni) however sullied by the sin of sodomy; of Filippo Argenti, a rich and haughty knight; of the Adimari family who, having acquired Dante's possessions at auction after his condemnation, had a special claim to the poet's resentment. This was the world of Cavalcante Cavalcanti, epicurean and nonbeliever in the next life, as perhaps was also his son Guido, intimate friend of Dante; of the usurer Gianni Baiamonte dei Becchi and the pimp Alessio Interminelli; of the barrator Bonturo Dati, who was head of the popular party in Lucca and exiled to Florence in the first years of the fourteenth century; of Frate Gomita, unfaithful vicar of Nino Visconti, prince of

Gallura; of Alighiero, Geri del Bello, a cousin of
Dante's father and counterfeiter like master Adamo,
vicar of the counts of Romena. This was also the world
of Griffolino di Arezzo, burned alive as an alchemist, a
fate like that of Capocchio Fiorentino who studied with
Dante and was sentenced to death in 1293; of the
epicurean and "spendthrift brigade" led by Caccia
d'Asciano, Stricca dei Salimbeni, Bartolommeo dei
Folcacchieri (l'Abbagliato), who were to represent a
large segment of the contemporary society in Florence,
Siena, and Lucca. This was the world of Vanni Fucci
of Pistoia, the sacrilegious thief whom Dante knew
personally in the war of Florence against Pisa; of
Cianfa Donati, also condemned as a thief and who
may have been one of Dante's relatives through his
wife; of Dante's friend, the lazy and slothful notary
Belacqua; of Buonconte da Montefeltro, Dante's com-
rade-in-arms, lost in the battle of Campaldino.[5] In
large part, therefore, the circles of the *Inferno* are
populated by Dante's contemporaries—people whom
he knew, among whom he lived, and with whom he
fought his political battles.

> Rejoice Florence, since you are so great that over
> land and over sea you beat your wings and your
> name is famous in Hell!

> (Godi Firenze, poichè se' sì grande
>   che per mare e per terra batti l'ali
>   e per l'inferno tuo nome si spande.)

5. For all references in the *Divina Commedia,* I have
made use of Natalino Sapegno's edition found in the collec-
tion "La Letteratura italiana, Storia e Testi," *4* (Milano-Napo-

Thus begins the canto describing the punishment of thieves and barrators (*Inferno,* XXVI). Although we can in part attribute the condemnation that Dante pronounced on many representatives of the times to political hatred and to a kind of moral retaliation against those who had branded him with charges of barratry and mismanagement of public funds, it is also true that specific documentary references exist attesting to the poet's close ties with the men and the affairs of his time. Thus, the allusion to one Ercolano Maconi, who might be identified with Lano fleeing from the battle of Pieve del Toppo (*Inferno,* XIII, 113), is confirmed by a document found in the archives of the Province of Siena concerning that very battle. Dante's reference to the dissipation of the spendthrift brigade, "in which Caccia d'Asciano squandered vineyard and forest" (in che disperse Caccia d'Asciano la vigna e la gran fronda) (*Inferno,* XXIX, 130), is confirmed, among other ways, by a deed in the abovementioned archives recalling Caccia's sale of land and farms to a certain Piccolomini. In these same archives there is preserved the list of expenditures executed by Capocchio and the entry of a twenty "soldi" fine charged to the musician Casella and to Cecco Angiolieri for going about the city at night, a sure sign of a dissipated and dissolute life. Even the vain search for the Diana waters (*Purgatorio,* XII, 151, 154) finds its proof in an adjudication of the General Council of the community of Siena in 1295, which allotted the

li, Riccardi). By using the Index of Names, it will be easy to trace the numerous passages cited above.

sum of seventy "librae" for reimbursement of the expenses incurred by the opera di Santa Maria in the search for those waters.[6]

Dante was very observant of the activities of his time, those of the lesser as well as the greater figures. Nor are the women of that day exempt from his condemnations, for feminine morals also determine, in large measure, the ethical fiber of each epoch's customs. As a contrast to the good Gualdrada, the daughter of Bellincion Berti and wife of Guido Guerra; Alagia, the niece of Adrian IV; and Forese Donati's widow Nella—all unusual examples of conjugal virtue—Dante pillories Enrico della Tosa's daughter Cianghella, who was famous for her immorality. For all his sympathetic understanding, he likewise condemns Francesca, obsessed by the fury of her passion and hatred for her killer husband. He has no qualms about hurling contemptuous sarcasm, through Forese's mouth, against the Florentine women "who expose their chest with their breasts" (che mostrano con le poppe il petto).

Nor are the upstarts spared his scorn—the Baldo d'Aguglione, the Fazio de' Mombaldini, and the Cerchi, whom the poet charged with having filled the cities with scoundrels through quick profits (subiti guadagni). He also accused them of being the source of the struggle between factions, while they were in fact the clearest evidence of the Florentine commune's

6. For the references on the various documents of the Archivio di Stato di Siena cited above, see Archivio di Stato di Siena, *Le Sala della Mostra e il Museo delle Tavolette dipinte* (Roma, 1956), pp. 117, 119, 120, and 124.

growing expansion and the great social change accompanying it.

One may also find proof in iconography of the poet's sharp observation of certain modes of expression particularly characteristic of his age. How, for example, can we fail to liken the obscene gesture of mockery that Vanni Fucci addresses to God to the allusion of Giannozzo Manetti, Mayor of Pistoia, who, in describing the city entrusted to his care, mentions the tower on the summit of which a sculptured arm was portrayed in the same obscene gesture directed toward Florence? With regard to the contest between Francesco and the devil for Guido da Montefeltro's soul, how can we fail to remember the bas-relief of the facade of St. Pietro, depicting the struggle between angel and demon on the deathbed, a popular topic for the sermons of the Mendicant Friars?

Dante was a keen and implacable witness of his age —keen in diagnosing a crisis, implacable in denouncing the moral degeneration at its source—even if, with all his moral reprobation, he could recognize the human values that many of those damned to eternal punishment or destined to the expiations of Purgatory had exemplified with unusual vigor. In this marked separation between the world of religious values and that of human ones is found perhaps one of the most significant points in Dante's ethical outlook.[7]

Brunetto Latini, who had guided Dante through the

7. Regarding Dante's understanding of human values, see Bruno Nardi's exemplary pages in *Dal Convivio alla Commedia* ("Sei saggi danteschi") in *Studi Storici* of the Istituto Storico Italiano per il Medioevo, Nos. 35–39 (Roma, 1960).

arduous path of learning "how man makes himself eternal" (come l'uom s'etterna) and who, under the Infernal rain of fire, reveals himself as still solicitous of the fate of his *Tesoro;* Farinata degli Uberti, still throbbing with partisan hatred and patriotic love; Cavalcante, who still recalls with accents of sorrowful nostalgia "the sweet light of earthly life" (lo dolce lume de la vita terrena) and still takes pride in the reputation of his son; Francesca, who, unsubdued by divine justice, vindicates the legitimacy of her sin in the name of love; Ulysses, exalted as the symbol of daring and human dignity in the quest for truth and valor—such figures as these, along with the encounters with Sordello, Bonagiunta da Lucca, and Casella, all still fervently participating in the human world of ideals, life, and art, are manifestations of the new spirit in which Dante viewed the world created by men as opposed to the world of grace and redemption created by God. For Dante there was no contradiction between these two worlds, or there would not have been save for the failure of the two highest powers to whom God had given the task of conciliating in one supreme synthesis the practice of earthly virtues, the quest for happiness and for universal peace, with the supreme aspirations of eternal salvation. That is why, in contrast to the description of contemporary society drawn from his personal experience, Dante took refuge in the nostalgic visions of Cacciaguida's era or of the first commune of Florence, when the "temperate and modest" (sobria e pudica) city was still concentrated within the first circle of its walls.

In those days the two suns shed their beneficent

light on the world. The cardinals and popes had not yet shown themselves to be more learned in the decretals than in the works of St. Augustine and the Church Fathers. Sts. Francis and Dominic had imparted new vigor to the ideals of the spiritual Church, and the Empire was adorned by figures such as those of Frederick II and Manfred, the former a heretic and the latter assuredly not free of sin. However, both were magnanimous and ready to sponsor the lofty and noble works undertaken in their courts, and they "followed human things, disdaining the bestial" (humana secuti, brutalia dedignantes).

Dante's nostalgic remembrance in exalting the good old days found a living voice in the words of Cacciaguida, the poet's ancestor, born in the early twelfth century and living at the time of Conrad III, and in those of Guido del Duca found in Canto XIV of the *Purgatorio.* In the *Paradiso,* Cacciaguida mentions with detachment—even though with the pride of a person belonging to one of the city's oldest families and related to the Elisei[8]—the rise of the first commune, just as Guido del Duca (*Purgatorio,* XIV, 109–11) reminisces about his own Romagna:

> The ladies and the knights, the toil and sports which love and courtesy made dear to us where hearts now have become so wicked.

> (Le donne e i cavalier, li affanni e li agi,
>   che ne 'nvogliava amore e cortesia
>   là dove i cuor son fatti sì malvagi.)

8. "Moronte and Eliseo were my brothers" (Moronte fu mio frate ed Eliseo—*Paradiso,* XV, 135).

In Cacciaguida's day Florence had approximately one-fifth of the number of citizenry fit to bear the arms that it had in Dante's time. If, as Villani tells us, the Florentines capable of bearing arms in the fourteenth century numbered around 30,000, in Cacciaguida's time they could have only slightly exceeded 6,000.[9] The Nerli, Vecchietti, Della Sannella, Dell'Arca, Soldanieri, Ardinghi, Bostichi, Ughi, Catellani, Filippi, Greci, Armanni, Alberighi, along with the Della Pressa, Galigai, Sacchetti, Giuochi, Fifanti, Barucci, Galli, Calpucci, Sizii, Lamberti, and Uberti (among whom the Della Pera, Nerli, Giandonati, Giangalandi, Pucci, Alepri, and Della Bella were conferred with knightly dignity) constituted the major lineages of the city, all dwelling within the circle of the first walls from the Baptistry of San Giovanni to the statue of Mars, situated at the beginning of the Ponte Vecchio before a flood swept it away in the Arno.

Women dressed modestly in those days, without gaudy ornaments or cosmetics. Their dowries, when they married, were not excessive; at home they tended to their children while working at the distaff and spinning wheel. They were not left widows prematurely through the absence of their husbands occupied in trading in the cities of Champagne and Flanders.

Bellincion Berti was the most celebrated representative of this world. Although he was one of the most prominent citizens, his belt was made of simple leather fastened by a buckle made of bone, and in winter he

9. A. Frugoni, "G. Villani, *Cronaca,* XI, 94," in *Bull. Istituto Storico Italiano per il Medioevo,* No. 76 (Roma, 1965).

wore raw (*scoverte*) pelts, that is to say, not lined with cloth or silk.

Afterwards, there descended upon Florence countrymen from Signa, Aguglione, Val di Greve, and Piviere d'Acone, all eager to become city-dwellers. Their grandparents had been peasants who went about begging in Simifonte; the grandchildren had in due course grown up "with an eye sharpened for bargaining" (con l'occhio aguzzo a barattare) through commerce and exchange. Without a doubt, Dante was alluding to the families of the Cerchi, Caponsacchi, Guidi, Infangati, Amidei, and Buondelmonti, who were of rural stock and recent fortune. The confusion of people and quick profits (confusione delle persone e i subiti guadagni) had corrupted the city, and the fratricidal quarrels that ultimately ruined Florence could be attributed directly to a certain Buondelmonti's murder by the Amidei over a broken marriage promise.[10]

Likewise Guido del Duca degli Onesti, noble and prudent man (nobilis vir prudens), a judge in Romagna in the mid-thirteenth century and related to the most prominent families of the region, tells of the decline of the dominant noble houses of his day. He uses as gloomy evidence the comparison between Rinieri dei Calboli of Forlì, Mayor of Faenza, Parma, and Ravenna from 1247 to 1292, valiant warrior and shrewd politician, and his grandson Fulcieri, Mayor of Florence in 1303, one of the leaders of the "Blacks" who raged like a wild beast against his "White" opponents.

10. For all references to the people cited, see Canto XVI of the *Paradiso*.

I see your grandson becoming a hunter of those
wolves on the shore of the fierce river and terrify-
ing them all.

(Io veggio tuo nepote che diventa
    cacciator di quei lupi in su la riva
    del fiero fiume, e tutti li sgomenta.)
                    (*Purgatorio,* XIV, 58–60)

If in his description of contemporary society, Dante
drew on his actual experience, from the hatreds and
loves, friendships and antipathies that helped to form
his own conscience as a noble citizen living in that
Florence bustling with economic and intellectual life,
but troubled with factious strife at the close of the
thirteenth century; if in reminiscing of the good old
days his vision lost its sense of reality, the figures of
magnanimous (*magnanimi*) personalities vaporized
into ideal types. Rather than individual names, the
generic names of entire families were used to characterize virtues or sins that, in the persons of Dante's
contemporaries relegated to the *Inferno* or the *Purgatorio,* were illuminated by the psychological observations appropriate to each person. Personalities and
families generically defined by a consensus of praise or
blame are contrasted to Ser Brunetto, Cavalcante,
Filippo Argenti, Vanni Fucci, and Belacqua—figures
fully sculptured and throbbing with life. The catalogs
of family names, so flattering to the municipal pride of
Cacciaguida, or Guido del Duca's exemplary citation
of the great race of lords from Romagna can be compared to the increasingly depersonalized figures of the

major protagonists of political and religious life in the last centuries of the Middle Ages, who populate the terraces of the *Purgatorio* or who shine with eternal light in the heavens of the *Paradiso*.

As a rule, Dante scholars cite the chronicles of Compagni and Villani, as well as the earliest commentators, in support of the poet's historical observations. However, Compagni was a contemporary of Dante, and the latter had no need to draw on the former for his references to events that constituted the common experience of political battles fought side by side. Moreover, he could not have known Villani's chronicles, which were being compiled at a time when the first cantos of the *Commedia* were already widely diffused through Florence and Central Italy. Dante could draw heavily on tradition, particularly for material concerning the immediately preceding generation. However, information on ancient Florence, the Swabians, principal events of the preceding century, and notable religious and political figures could have come only from literary sources. Although he does not cite them, Dante undoubtedly must have known and made use of them because he often presupposes the story and comments on its meaning with words closely following the original text.

Forty years ago, in a work published on the anniversary of Dante's death and based on an antecedent work of Busson, I attempted to show that the source of many of the most famous Dantesque episodes—particularly those referring to the period of struggle between the Swabians and the Papacy and to the oldest history of the Florentine commune—was the *Cronaca* of Ricordano Malispini.[11] Now that the authenticity of that chronicle is widely acknowledged, with general recognition of the use Villani made of it in his work prior to 1282, the fact that Malispini inspired Dante has no need of further documentation.[12] His influence is seen not only in episodes and figures of whom Dante could have had no direct knowledge but also in the spirit which chronicler and poet shared, both cherishing the happy and incorrupt days of the city from which their contemporaries had estranged themselves.

The Guelf Ricordano Malispini, who had been banished from Florence after the Battle of Montaperti and who probably, after having been a guest of his relatives, the Capocci, in Rome, had followed the vicissitudes of the times culminating in the downfall of the Swabians, lived approximately one century after Cacciaguida's day. However, he shared the latter's ideals and, like him, greatly admired the chivalrous Guelf

11. "Dante, il Villani e Ricordano Malispini," in *Bull. dell'Istituto Storico Italiano,* No. 41 (1921).

12. For the whole question on Malispini, other than my own studies, see "Note malispiniane," "Dante, il Villani e Ricordano Malispini," and "Ancora sulla questione malispiniana," in *Bull. dell'Istituto Storico Italiano* (1920, 1921, and 1930). See also E. Sicardi, "Due Cronache del Vespro in volgare siciliano del sec. XIII," in *Rer. Ital. Scriptores,* new ed. Carducci & Fiorini, Accessiones novissimae, Nos. 157–58 (Bologna, 1917), and more recently, A. del Monte, "La Storiografia fiorentina del Trecento: Ricordano Malispini, Dino Compagni e Giovanni Villani," in *Secoli vari,* Conferenze della Libera Cattedra di Storia della Civiltà Fiorentina (Firenze, Sansoni). For the authenticity of Ricordano Malispini's *Cronaca,* see also Hans Nabholz, *Einführung in das Studium der mitt. und der neueren Geschichte* (Zurich, 1948).

traditions of the original Florence. Dante heard in him the voice of that tradition recalling the first great families of Florence, enumerating them, like Cacciaguida, with painstaking diligence, district by district, indicating the houses and origins of each, while with aristocratic disdain he mentioned the names of the nouveaux riches, "who were then barely on the rise" (che erano allora di picciolo cominciamento), and who were later to grow in influence through commerce and the arts. In Malispini, Dante could find passages deploring the quarrels among the citizens and a detailed account of the murder of Buondelmonte de' Buondelmonti, which was for the chronicler, as for the poet, the unhappy origin of those quarrels. Dante could also find the allusions to that saga of the Swabians that constitutes one of the salient motifs in his historical evocation of the age preceding his own. In Ricordano, who wrote after 1270 and who, *laudator temporis acti* like all old men, described the Florence of his grandfathers, Dante could read the details of the sober and decent lives of the Florentine men of Bellincion Berti's time and later put the words in Cacciaguida's mouth. In Malispini, the past lived again as a lament for the days of youth and the hopeful time of life when family, party, and city were in their flowering stage.

On the contrary, in Villani's *Cronaca* can be seen the pride of a Florence which has reached the apex of its splendor, the "Uccellatoio" (Florence) which "in its ascent" (nel suo montare) had already surpassed "Montemalo" (Rome) which was "in its decline" (nel suo calare). In Villani's recollection the past faded away into a colorless narrative, without the political notations that Malispini had supplied.

For Dante, looking toward the future in a dream of peace and justice, the past represented the moral justification for his disgust with the present. For this, he found an ideal concurrence in Malispini, one he could not have found in Villani, the great merchant of the "Compagnia dei Peruzzi," a member of the oligarchy of bankers, the man who had taken over the reins of government in Florence after the fall of the "White's" commune and who, being on familiar terms with Europe's major political figures, had shaped the course of many of the major political events of that epoch.[13]

The Florence in which Villani took pride—the Florence which dominated the European markets with its production of quality textiles; whose bankers lent money to the pontiffs and kings of the major European powers and who were, in the words of Boniface VIII, the fifth element of the universe, grand lords, ambassadors, and advisers to those in power; the city of world-wide importance which, precisely because of Dante, Petrarch, and Boccaccio, the great triad of the fourteenth century, was preparing to become the cradle of the Italian vernacular and of the civilization of the forthcoming Renaissance—held no positive values for Dante. The dream of a universal Empire, of a Church regenerated and brought back to the pure exercise of her spiritual functions, of states and cities in peace and accord, sustained by the justice of princes

13. F. P. Luiso, "Indagini biografiche su Giovanni Villani," in *Bull. Istituto Storico Italiano per il Medioevo*, No. 51 (1936).

and directed toward the exaltation of the most noble human activities, made the reality of the time pale and meaningless to the eyes of the poet. Against the degenerate Florence, infested with that "ungrateful wicked populace" (ingrato popolo maligno) descended from the beasts of Fiesole and from the immigrants of the countryside, Dante did not hesitate to invoke the vengeance and punishment of the ineffective Henry VII.

Such is the judgment that Dante passed on the world and on the Florence of his day, an objective, often pitiless verdict not always free of resentment and of partisan hatred. At the same time, it is inspired, as is apparent in the contrast to the ideal world and the good old days, by the highest social and religious concepts. It is for this reason that, whether or not his judgment on the society of his time was fundamentally lacking in a sense of history or influenced by contingent passion, and whether or not his dream was destined to vanish into a Utopian sky, the poet's moral and social message, set forth in a work of art revealing the deepest meaning of the Middle Ages, has preserved its validity through the centuries.

3.

Dante and Thirteenth-Century Asceticism

BY GIORGIO PETROCCHI

*Professor of Italian Language and Literature,
University of Rome*

Dante's ascetics, taking into consideration his cultural
and devotional interest and his tastes as a reader and
thirteenth-century man, may be assigned a place next
to his mystical experience. We must all reject the facile
and convenient theory of a Dantesque syncretism assimilating and justifying the conflicts and resolutions
of the thought of his own age and the immediately
preceding one; however, it is also true that the spiritual
outlook of the *Commedia* can be identified by the
parallel process of mystical-ascetical, and apocalyp-
tical-messianic influences. The first influence finds expression in the passionate and purposeful "journey to
God" (itinerarium in Deum) and may be traced to
Bernardian, Victorian, and Bonaventurian mystical
theology, while the latter influence draws on the
Joachimite and Celestinian postures of expectation
and invocation of God's emissary, the renewer of
mankind and restorer of the Church.

GIORGIO PETROCCHI

It is not my intention to repeat or, if it were possible, to supplement previous investigations into what Dante gained from his reading of those mystics and prophets, although defining his nucleus of personal ascetics (especially on the topic of the purgation of sins) could involve authors and theological areas pertaining to mystics. Nor will I trespass on medieval prophetism with its stress on poverty and charity. We can say that, even on the structural or allegorical plane, although obeying purely literary exigencies, the two poles of attraction in Dante's spirituality have fomented interest in reading the text with close attention to the components which touch on the mystical process. Take for example Singleton's pages on the "pattern at the center" and the "substance of things seen," or the impressions of mystical experience in the concept of Christian allegory found in Auerbach's equally famous pages. Moreover, inquiry into Dante as the "scribe of God" (scriba Dei) compromises the resolution of the case proposed to us by Sarolli regarding the sources of inspiration and the objective method of presentation first of the "Veltro," then of the "Five-hundred-ten-and-five" (Cinquecento diece e cinque—DXV), and finally of the poet's self-denomination as the prophet-renewer of mankind.[1]

To be sure, the ascetic exigency was not extraneous to the message of Gioacchino da Fiore, either in that

1. See in particular, C. Singleton's *Studi su Dante, 1* (Napoli, 1961); E. Auerbach's *Studi su Dante* (Milano, 1963); and G. R. Sarolli's "Dante 'scriba Dei,'" *Convivium,* 6 (1963). Also consult K. Foster's essay, "Dante as a Christian Poet," in *God's Tree: Essays on Dante and Other Matters* (London, 1957).

ardent zeal for purity and sacrifice generically char-
acterizing the religious temperament of Giovanni
Lotario's age and propagated by St. Francis throughout the thirteenth century, or in the central teaching
of the Lenten Cycle, which was "endurance in work
and weeping" through a hard penitential experience as
a preparation for the Holy Spirit. This leads to identifying the second age—which the "Calabrian abbot"
affirmed mankind was living through—with the age
of tribulation and suffering preparing the human spirit
for the forthcoming joy of rebirth in the Holy Ghost.

I am not among those inclined to recognize the easy
parallels of figures and allegorical situations as between Joachim and Dante, and I believe that Barbi's
warning against the identification of Dante's prophetic
theme with the Joachimite vision both in the *Liber
figurarum,* insofar as it may be attributed to him, and
the *Concordia novi ac veteris Testamenti* is still valid
today.[2] Yet one cannot dismiss as alien to Dante's
thinking the influence of that apocalyptical ferment
which the environment of the spirituali had borrowed
from "gioachimismo." Within such limits and taking
care not to cross them recklessly—that is, not to stray
from the precise content of the texts—Dante received a
powerful stimulus from medieval prophetism through
the polemics of pauperism against the "relaxati" and in
a politico-religious sphere as well as in a sphere of
purely personal ascetic pursuit, culminating in the

2. See M. Barbi in *Studi Danteschi, 33* (1958) 35 ff.
Concerning Gioacchino and Dante, see, above all, L. Ton-
delli, *Da Gioacchino a Dante* (Torino, 1944) and "Rassegna
gioachimita-dantesca," *Sophia, 19* (1951); E. Buonaiuti, *La
prima rinascita* (Varese, 1952).

exhortation to purification in expectation of the divine vengeance. The poet's purpose matures within that complex of penitential admonitions which must be kept clearly in mind if one wishes to understand something about the thirteenth-century Franciscan movement, the Alleluia movement, the heterodox legacies from the Arnaldiani to the Umiliati, down to the great pages of the Umbrian Discipline. One must also bear in mind the resumption of all these motives within the Minorite family, thanks to the leaders of the spiritual faction (above all, such spirituali as Gerardo da S. Donnino and Giovanni da Parma, who in their Founder identified the angel of the sixth seal of the Apocalypse) and to the poet, Jacopone da Todi.

We might find place here for the controversial but fascinating topic of Celestino V, whose presence or nonpresence in the vestibule of the Dantesque Inferno does not rightly belong to this discussion, but there is the obligation to mention his evident Joachimite filiation both directly and through the spirituali in the analogous resolution to remake himself affirmed in an ascetic message of a marked "contempt for the world." Pietro del Morrone, upon ascending to the Papacy, took the name of Celestino II, who, one hundred years before, had set aside all the objections to the approval of Joachim da Fiore's hermetic order. Pietro's attitude is related to the prophetical-messianic theme we have considered collateral to the thought of the thirteenth-century ascetics—associating or separating the angelic Pope, eagerly awaited by the "giachomiti" and the Dantesque Veltro insofar as the authority called upon to cleanse the world—He Who will restore justice and evangelical love to tormented mankind—is indeed always "an awakener of those who are sleeping" (excubitor dormitantium), a sower of the ascetic spirit.

However, another circumstance is central to our theory—the fact that Celestino V is both "cursed and lamented" in Dante, passionately longed for on the eve of the 1294 Conclave in Perugia and excessively execrated on the morrow of the "great refusal." Yet, he founded a religious order rigorously influenced by the Benedictine rule but kindling the penitential spirit of his monks from Maiella with Franciscan pauperism which gave substance and meaning to Benedictine anchoretism. However much we may be inclined to see it as repudiated, this Celestinian asceticism had entered into Dante's blood and that of the men of his generation, including his beloved Charles Martel; and certain ideals that enter into the soul of a young man can never be cast out (and this particular young man, we might add, precisely in 1294 was terminating his Franciscan studies in St. Croce where he was nourished on the doctrine of the spirituali).

However, the mystic and prophet of the *Commedia* have relegated the ascetic to the shadows, or at least the latter has a kind of subordinate status with respect to the very marked emphasis on the mystic vision (visio) and the proclaimed reformatory mission of the voyage into the beyond. After all, Dante is not at fault—and less so we who study him—if there still remain some theologians who consider asceticism complementary to mysticism, at least in the special concept of the "path of perfection" (cammino di perfezione) followed under the impulse of the common means of grace.

Viewed in its external prospect the *Commedia* is a report defective in its last part, of one who is "carried away" (raptus). The character Dante is snatched from the earth under the influence of those psychic phenomena of exceptional character that present themselves, for the most part, as determinants of the mystic state, i.e. ecstasy. But this ecstasy—observe in what conflict with the laws of eschatological literature the enraptured one finds himself—is not immediate; it is a gradual process with successive sensual manifestations. Dante always cooperates, not only in the *Inferno* where he feels sorrow and pity, suffers fatigue, falls asleep— the enraptured sleep is not unknown to mystics—and in the second *cantica,* but also in the *Paradiso,* where his collaboration is active, for the sweetness of the sounds pleases his ear and his sight is gladdened by the colors of the blessed and the celestial spheres.

If we were to subject this observation to an analysis of mystical typology, the report would be simple enough: Dante (the analyst would reply) is not a mystic in the strict sense but a man of letters who has claimed for himself, for the convenience of a rhetorical project and through love of a literary form in common use at the time, an experience never truly lavished upon him by God. In effect, Dante is only rarely in that state of mind called apathy; he is not the passive object of the total and free action of God except in the vision of the Empyrean which is, however, conceived, even in terms of the narrative, as a vision seen from afar, as an admirable but detached contemplation. He reaches it by disposing his soul, through his own efforts, to receive the supernatural effusion of Grace. However, at the moment that such an exceptional gift is given him, the poem ends, stopping abruptly with the customary excuse of the ineffability of the vision of God.

To conclude, the *Commedia* is a mystical poem that lacks its substantial part, a tragedy without its fifth act—either because Dante wished to conceive the conclusion of the mystical process as a full union in God with the annihilation of every human distraction, or because he thought of it rather as a transformative vision. We cannot be sure, since Dante pretends not to remember what he has experienced—as if he could not have found in the pages of the Benedictine and Franciscan mystics so dear to him sufficient material for writing a thirty-fourth and even a thirty-fifth canto of the *Paradiso*.

The truth is otherwise; Dante did indeed conceive the general structure of the poem as a mystical account, but he did not want to carry the narrative fiction beyond a certain limit, that is, past the initial stage of the Beatific Vision. The cause of this prudence in the mystic is to be sought in the necessities of the ascetic. Here is the origin, the formation, the elaboration of the rich ascetic theme of the *Commedia*. Man is hesitant, with a deep but confused perception of the sin that has stained him. He aspires to redeem himself but does not have sufficient energy to do so. Within the mystic story there is the report—detailed, sincere, without calculated overtones, and with full identification of the character with Dante, the man and the poet—of an earthly experience symbolized, reflected, or hypothesized in the various vicissitudes and encounters in the course of the eschatological pilgrimage.[3]

3. This is Dante's "earthly" (terreno) voyage to which Singleton recently recalled us (preface to *Studi su Dante*,

The source, as usual, is St. Thomas Aquinas. It will be worth our while to study together the ascetic schema that he drew up in the *Summa Theologiae* (II–II, q. 24, art. 9) and to verify in what way Dante applied it to the *Commedia*—a verification that I believe has never been made—in terms of the three phases of ascetic perfection that are fulfilled through the three stages of love, "following diverse pursuits, to which man is led through an increase in love" (secundum diversa studia, ad quae homo perducitur per charitatis augmentum).

The first phase of perfection is that of the "principiants" (principianti). It consists in the task of abandoning sin (ad recedendum a peccato) and suppressing the passions, above all concupiscence, "and in resisting those [passions of] concupiscence that are contrary to charity" (et resistendum concupiscentiis eius, quae in contrarium charitatis movent). From the principiants we pass to the "progressors" (progredienti), as it were, from the purgative to the enlightened path, in expectation of the unitive one; progress in goodness under charitable impulse sets in motion all the virtues. Finally, there is the third phase belonging to the "Perfect" (perfecti), namely, those who, having subjugated their passions and overcome sin, "wish to be set free and to be with Christ" (cupiunt dissolvi et esse cum Christo) according to St. Paul; in them is the zeal "to be changed in the greatest degree to the end, that they may be a

---

pp. 11–12): "The literary event of Dante's voyage into the next world recalls to mind a type of earthly voyage" (l'evento letterale di un viaggio di Dante al di là di questa vita richiama alle mente l'evento di una specie di viaggio terreno).

part of God" (circa hoc maxime versatur ut Deo in-
haerent).

While it would be rash to see a correspondence between the three phases of ascetic perfection and the
three parts of the *Commedia,* it must be recognized that
the *Inferno* presents a series of spiritual exercises related not only to the observation of sin and its consequences in the place of damnation, but also to the
repugnance aroused by vice, to the rejection of the sinful act. Dante, taking leave of the sodomites or fleeing
from the barrators, has not only identified the evil but
has begun to free himself from it in various but always
positive ways—with scorn or pity (Filippo Argenti or
Francesca), or by reasoning about it, or by feeling
shaken.

In short, detachment from sin in the continuing path
of perfection creates and develops a rather advanced
ascetic scale which is not confined to the experimental
consciousness of God's justice but is a horror of sin
in all its manifestations. It is therefore a declaration of
love of the Supreme Good (Sommo Bene) and a rein-
forced yearning for virtue; for the beauty of creation
("When Divine love/first moved those beautiful
things" [Quando l'amor divino/mosse di prima quelle
cose belle]); for the Divine properties ("The Divine
Power/the Supreme Wisdom and the Primal Love"
[la divina potestate,/la somma sapienza e 'l primo
amore]); and for the gift of redemption ("a mighty
one/crowned with the mark of victory" [un possente,/
con segno di vittoria coronato]).

That the ascetic process is in full development in the
Purgatorio is a point so evident we need not linger

upon it—from the liturgical initiation of the first canto, to the revival of the "stunned virtue" (tramortita virtù), through "the sweet draught that would never have sated me" (lo dolce ber che mai non m'avria sazio), and thence, in addition to being "prepared to mount to the stars" (disposto a salire alle stelle), being fundamentally "remade . . . pure" (rifatto . . . puro).

Defining the ascetics of the *Paradiso* may seem more difficult in that the ascetic experience is constantly accompanied by contemplation. However, we can say that insofar as Dante longs to drink from the fountain of Divine Grace and foretastes—for the future when he can return, if worthy, to those blessed heavenly spheres—the joy of belonging to God, he enjoys all the rewards of the unitive path and therefore brings to completion his "ascetic journey." Insofar as he is allowed to contemplate the immensity of Divine works in relation to man, the modes and grades of celestial beatitude, and finally the mysteries of the Divine Essence, he finds himself in the highest stage of infused contemplation and therefore at the end of his "mystical journey."

However, in the poetic act, that is to say, when we propose to interpret and evaluate the contents of the *Paradiso,* Dante's experiences can be differentiated only in the abstract, since he does not wish to feel God's presence in a moment distinct from the time he is admitted to contemplate Him, and therefore he feels Him within himself. Besides, we should remember that Dante did not limit himself to St. Thomas' schema but also intended to appeal to the intellective and sensitive faculties that Bonaventure held essential for contemplation, prayer, meditation, and the quest not for earthly serenity but for the supreme peace of the soul nearing its return to the Creator. St. Bonaventure writes: "Whoever wishes to ascend to God must ascend above himself through the universe which is the stairway to God, by means of an ascetics of the soul exercising natural powers: sense, imagination, reason, intellect, the apex of the mind" (Chiunque vuol ascendere a Dio è necessario che ascenda al di sopra di se stesso, attraverso l'universo che è scala a Dio, per una ascesi dell'anima, esercitando le naturali potenze: senso, immaginazione, ragione, intelletto, apice della mente). The complex of stimuli received by Dante all the way from the forest to the Empyrean, making him increasingly cognizant of sin and virtue, is all implied within these "natural powers." I leave it to you to decide whether in the *Commedia* the pilgrim's intellect is more important than his feelings and imagination— even if we limit our consideration to the religious component of the "sacred poem"—which, as you know, never find emotional or unpremeditated expression.

Yet another element must be added, one permitting us to clarify the importance which this ascetic process has for the understanding of the lines of development running through the poem.[4] The gift allowing Dante to see the triple realm while still alive is not presented as a concession whose sole end is to free the poet from the dangers of the savage forest. At least it will not be seen as such once the idea of the Dantesque mission

4. I have previously discussed this in "Itinerari nella Commedia," *Studi Danteschi, 41* (1964). See especially the part relating to the "mystic journey" (itinerario mistico).

becomes more clear as the poem proceeds. It is a charisma, a boon granted with the general welfare in mind, given to an individual in order that he may show men the straight path, that the Church may return to her evangelical mission, that peace and justice may once more triumph on earth, that mankind may redeem itself.

The ascetic experience must therefore assume the form of a conventional treatise containing the rules for shunning sin and preparing the soul for eternal salvation. The charismatic miracle of being third, after Aeneas and Paul, justifies that real structure of didactic poetry that the *Commedia* aspires to have, even accepting the ultimate consequences of scholastic encyclopedism. It is the third heavenly (*paradisiaco*) degree that Dante strives to attain; there he is simultaneously wayfarer, understanding pupil, and teacher. He is still a pilgrim on earth but has already arrived in his celestial homeland; from below and from on high he can exhort mankind to self-renewal. Just as writers of treatises use fictitious characters to create the assumptions of the philosophical discussion—"thus it is advanced . . . but against it is . . . I answer saying" (sic proceditur . . . sed contra est . . . respondeo dicendum)—so too, and so much the better, the poet entrusts the teaching function to characters other than himself, the protagonist, precisely because he is a "wayfarer."

If, therefore, the ascetic outline is substantially a particular version of Thomism, the specific quality of the moral experience is Franciscan with regard both to the concrete tenets of the saint's *Regula* and *Testa-*

mentum and to the "interpretation" of the spirituali or to the concept of the Church's "new order." St. Francis, dying, had entreated that no gloss be made on the text of his rule; but no disciple can fail to feel the necessity of interpretation. Dante accepts in part the gloss of the spirituali, even though he criticizes (*Paradiso,* XII, 124–31) the excessive doctrinal rigidity of some positions, particularly that of Ubertino, who "coerces" (coarta) the rule. But even if there had been insufficient political motives to justify this stand (the solidarity of comrades in the struggle against Boniface VIII), or if the closeness of the youthful years to the poverty-stricken apostolate of Olivi were of no worth, we would still have to reckon with the decisive factor of Dante's religious sentiment, rigorous and pugnacious, sympathetic to "saintly athletes." All the most thoughtful readers of the eleventh canto of the *Paradiso* have felt this, from Auerbach to Nardi and Bosco: the Francis lauded by Aquinas is above all the spouse of Lady Poverty, the inflexible and austere advocate of individual poverty ("and before his spiritual court/ and before his father, he was united to her" [e dinanzi a la sua spirital corte/et coram patre le si fece unito]) and of conventual poverty ("the venerable Bernard/ first bared his feet," "Egidius bared his feet, Sylvester his," "that little family/girded already by the humble cord" ['l venerabile Bernardo/si scalzò prima . . . Scalzasi Egidio, scalzasi Silvestro . . . quella famiglia/che già legava l'umile capestro]).

Since it is clear we are now in an area in the main ascetic, we may note that Franciscan poverty does not serve only to depict a scene in the life of its Founder; it colors, in fact, the entire *Commedia,* as is evident in the invectives against the she-wolf and avarice and the fervid assertions of the purity and sobriety of the old Florentines, or the friars and monks of yore, or "sweet Maria" (dolce Maria), or "good Fabrizio" (buon Fabrizio):

> Be accursed, ancient wolf, you who have more prey than any other beast because of your endlessly ravenous hunger!
> O Heavens! through whose revolutions people believe that conditions here below are changed, when will someone come to drive it away?

> (Maladetta sie tu, antica lupa,
>   che più di tutte l'altre bestie hai preda
>   per la tua fame sanza fine cupa!
> O ciel, nel cui girar par che si creda
>   le condizion di qua giù trasmutarsi,
>   quando verrà per cui questa disceda?)
>   (*Purgatorio,* XX, 10–15)

Moreover, once it is established that the theme of repudiation of earthly goods, with the consequent disdain of greed for them, shows traces of the Franciscan message and the gloss of Observance (Osservanza)— all of which can be found in the framework of the preceding Benedictine tradition, particularly among the Cistercians—it follows that an ascetic motif of fundamental importance is ever present in the spiritual aspect of the *Commedia.* We see it affirmed as central in the initial verses, "and which has in the past made many live in sorrow" (e molte genti fè già viver grame); definitively sealed in St. Peter Damian's apostrophe; glorified in the final exaltation of the Poor Little Man (Poverello) in the glory of the Empyrean; and radiated in a series of minor constellations, all of Franciscan stamp—from the ecstatic and excited contemplation of the beauty of creation to the profound aspiration toward an austere, absolute, and unshakable faith.

If we shift from the direct teaching of St. Francis to the poverty-oriented if not politico-ecclesiastical doctrine of the spirituali, the picture, rather than diminishing in size, grows larger with the addition of moral ferment and polemic exhortations with respect to the concept of the Church of the future, the "spiritual" Church (Ecclesia spiritualis), which is not exactly the Church of the spirituali but is at any rate the Church of the poor, or the one which gives its goods to the poor. The names of Clareno, Olivi, and even the disparaged Ubertino stand beside that of Jacobo de Tuderte to aid us in the understanding of the disdains and hopes in the *Convivio, Monarchia,* and the *Epistole,* as well as those set forth in the *Commedia.*

> Yet the wound will be healed (though it cannot be otherwise than that the brand and scar of infamy will have been burned with fire upon the Apostolic See, and will disfigure her for whom heaven and earth had been reserved), if ye, who were the authors of this transgression, will all with one accord fight manfully for the Bride of Christ, for the Throne of the Bride, which is

Rome, for our Italy, and that I may speak more
fully, for the whole commonwealth of pilgrims
upon the earth; so that from the palestra where
the contest has already begun, and which is gazed
upon from all the shores of the ocean, ye fighting
gloriously may hear, "Gloria in excelsis!"[5]

(*Emendabitur quidem—quanquam non sit quin
nota cicatrix infamis Apostolicam Sedem usque
ad ignem, cui celi qui nunc sunt et terra sunt
reservati, deturpet—, si unanimes omnes qui
huiusmodi exorbitationis fuistis auctores, pro
Sponsa Christi, pro sede Sponsa que Roma est,
pro Ytalia nostra, et ut plenius dicam, pro tota
civitate peregrinante in terris, viriliter propug-
netis, ut de palestra iam cepti certaminis undique
ab Occeani margine circumspecta, vosmetipsos
cum gloria offerentes, audire possitis: "Gloria in
excelsis."*)

The ascetic schema is based on the concept of the
excellence and primacy of charity, in that it is the form
of all the other virtues and the efficient mode of the
search for God. But is the God of the *Commedia* the
earthly Love of the ascetic or the abstract Love of the
theologian and mystic? In the continuity and contiguity
of the poetic images representing God, readers have

5. The translation used is that by Charles Sterrett
Latham, *A Translation of Dante's Eleven Letters,* ed. George
Rice Carpenter (Boston, Houghton, Mifflin & Co., 1892),
p. 173. The quotation is from Dante's "Letter to the Italian
Cardinals."

been inclined to find Him an abstraction or perhaps to find themselves in the presence of a

> celestial God, almost an omnipotent force, inaccessible, faceless and nameless, Who does not awaken storms or calms of affection but [only] a surprised and bewildered adoration. In brief, more a biblical than an evangelical God, more apocalyptic than Pauline, an enigmatic reality, superhuman and slightly inhuman—for that aspect which It sometimes assumes of an existence "demonstrated according to the methods of geometry."

> (Dio celeste, quasi una forza onnipotente, inaccessibile, senza volto e senza nome, che non desta tempeste e calme di affetti ma solo una stupefatta e smarrita adorazione. Insomma un Dio biblico, più che un Dio evangelico, un Dio apocalittico più che un Dio paolino, una realtà sfingea, sovrumana e un po' disumana—per quell' aspetto che talora assume di una esistenza "more geometrico demonstrata.")[6]

However, in the context of God's pronouncements and given the character of Beatrice's lectures—and those of all the other instructors in the third *cantica*—what other image of the Father could find expression? Actually, if we want to come down to a definition possibly indefensible not only on scriptural grounds but also as exegesis of the poem, the God of the

6. Giovanni Getto, "Il Canto XXIX del *Paradiso*," in *Letture dantesche* (Firenze, Sansoni, 1962), p. 1, 941.

Paradiso is reminded of His fatherly love, from which flows the supreme essence of love and which creates new sources of love in the angels: "the Eternal Love disclosed Itself in new loves" (s'aperse in nuovi amor l'etterno amore).

More clearly than elsewhere we find set forth in Canto XXIX the identification of God and love; it is here that the poet defines, in words of high poetic tension, the strict relation between the act of the intellective vision of Divinity insofar as it is brought about by the presence of illuminating grace, and the act of love:

> Therefore, since affection follows the act of conceiving [the vision of God], the joy of loving glows variously, greater or less, in them.

> (Onde, però che a l'atto che concepe
> segue l'affetto, d'amar la dolcezza
> diversamente in essa ferve e tepe.)

The "first goodness, which is God" (prima bontade, che è Dio), as Dante writes in the *Convivio,* extends infinitely over the celestial creatures whose fervor of love for the Creator varies in proportion with the intensity of their vision of God. The concept is expressed in terms of absolute doctrinal rigor, but without any enigmatic or inhuman qualities and therefore without any interpretations that can apply, comparatively, to God; the concept obviously cannot contain elements of approximation to humanity or separation from it and is both clarity and mystery.

Dante's voyage in the third realm may be compared

to an incessant effort to draw near to the "light" (luce) and "mystery" (mistero). On the one hand comes the lyric fulfillment of images shining in an intense or blazing splendor. These are images that find their first literary formulation in various parts of the *Convivio* (the treatise that must have represented for Dante, among other things, a most efficacious stylistic apprenticeship for giving lifeblood and color to his doctrinal imagination, to his rhetorical domination of his concepts): "And so . . . we are now to discourse of the spiritual sun, accessible to the intellect, that is God"[7] (Cosi' e' ora da ragionare, per lo sole spirituale e intelligibile, che e' Iddio), which later ends in the final contemplation, "O Eternal Light abiding in Thyself alone" (O luce etterna che sola in te sidi).

On the other hand, the full awareness of the inscrutable divine mystery is responsible for the repeated affirmations of the pilgrim Dante regarding the ineffability and mystery of predestination and the Divine acts, until it culminates in the ample confession of Canto XIX:

> Consequently the sight your world receives penetrates into eternal justice as the eye penetrates within the sea; for, although at the shore the bottom is seen, on the main it is not, and nevertheless the bottom is there, its depth hiding it. No light unless it comes from the Serene One is always

7. The translation used is that by Philip H. Wicksteed, *The Convivio of Dante Alighieri,* Temple Classics Edition (London, J. M. Dent & Co., 1909), p. 203. The text is from *Convivio,* III, 12.

untroubled, but dark is that shadowed by the flesh
and its poison.

> (Però ne la giustizia sempiterna
>   la vista che riceve il vostro mondo
>   com'occhio per lo mare, entro s'interna;
> che, ben che da la proda veggia il fondo,
>   in pelago nol vede; e nondimeno
>   ègli, ma cela lui l'esser profondo.
> Lume non è, se non vien dal sereno
>   che non si turba mai; anzi è tenebra,
>   od ombra de la carne, o suo veleno.)
>   (*Paradiso,* XIX, 58–66)

That the reading of St. Paul has rendered more precise the images of Divine charity is an indubitable
fact, and it would be rash to compare or simply detect
a Johannine and Pauline God in the *Paradiso.* We
would find an abundance and, indeed, a superfluity of
quotations. But I would like to mention here the concrete application of Dante, the simple translator of
that Paul who is not even a "direct" character in the
Paradiso but who is vulgarized in the *Convivio* in one
of the parts most useful to our case—"Oh height of
the wealth of the wisdom of God, how incomprehen-
sible are thy judgments and thy ways past finding out"[8]
(O altezze de le divizie de la sapienza di Dio, come sono
incomprensibili li tuoi giudicii e investigabili le tue vie)
(*Convivio,* IV, 21, 6)—and on whom Dante clearly
relies in the often repeated theme of the "Prime Goodness" (prima bonitas):

8. (Translator's note.) Wicksteed, p. 331.

The Divine Goodness which spurns all envy, burning in Itself, so shines that It sends forth Its eternal beauty.

> (La divina bontà, che da sé sperne
> ogni livore, ardendo in sé, sfavilla
> sì che dispiega le bellezze etterne.)
> *(Paradiso,* VII, 64–66)

In Canto VII, this concept is immediately recalled in the line coming a little later than the passage just quoted—"The Divine Goodness which puts Its stamp on the world" (La divina bontà che 'l mondo imprenta) —and in the passionate and energetic exhortation of Canto X, marked by a solemn and quasi-liturgical rhythm:

Gazing at His Son with the Love which both eternally breathe forth, the first and ineffable Power.

> (Guardando nel suo Figlio con l'Amore
> che l'uno e l'altro etternalmente spira,
> lo primo ed ineffabile Valore.)
> *(Paradiso,* X, 1–3)

Prepared by an unending series of such spiritual as well as doctrinal definitions, the reader learns to observe the diversity of tone between the exhortations of astronomical-scientific nature and those of poetic figures, as in Canto XXIX:

Not to acquire any benefit for Itself, which cannot be, but in order that Its splendor might declare as It shines "I am," the Eternal Love, in its eternity, outside of Time and every other limitation, as It pleased, disclosed Itself in new loves.

(Non per avere a sé di bene acquisto,
   ch'esser non può, ma perché suo splendore
   potesse, risplendendo, dir "Subsisto,"
in sua etternità di tempo fore,
   fuor d'ogni altro comprender, come i piacque,
   s'aperse in nuovi amor l'etterno amore.)

(ll. 13–18)

The terzine draw their significance from the combination of the light image, "splendor . . . shining" (splendore . . . risplendendo), with that of infinite temporal extension. This significance becomes further enriched in the subsequent terzina and draws its energetic and expressive drive from the closing verse: "the moving of God over these waters" (lo discorrer di Dio sovra quest'acque).

Of the dramatis personae of this grandiose ascetic drama, formulated as a medieval representation of soul and body (d'anima et de corpo), we have seen the two principal actors—God-Love and the sinner Dante, the terminal point and motive cause of the process of penitence and purification from sin.

If we wish to come down to a specific typological inquiry, the reading of the *Purgatorio* offers a complete series of particular cases, whether it be considered an objectification of moral questions reflecting the poet's personal ascetics or an example of a moral reality which has no concrete relationship to the protagonist's spirituality but which completes or fills in the framework of theological casuistry. This is accomplished by the didactic design of the second *cantica,* through the Shades "suffering diverse anguish" (disparmente angosciate) in their effort to regain their native purity, "purging the mist of the world" (purgando la caligine del mondo).

Dante is too varied a narrator to make us always witness the same interpretation of his role as a purgatorial pilgrim—for he himself must undergo the same sufferings as the souls whom he encounters, and appropriate to the departments in which he finds himself. For example, among the envious, the wayfarer's personal ascetics condense into an impulse of intense compassion, and such an impulse fulfills his own obligation as a penitent.

> I do not believe a man lives today so hard that he would not be touched by pity for what I then saw, for when I had arrived so close to them that their features became clear, grief brought tears to my eyes.

> (Non credo che per la terra vada ancoi
>   omo sì duro, che non fosse punto
>   per compassion di quel ch'i' vidi poi;
> ché, quando fui sì presso di lor giunto
>   che li atti loro a me venivan certi,
>   per li occhi fui di greve dolor munto.)
>   (*Purgatorio,* XIII, 52–57)

Neither "the odor of an apple" (l'odor di un pomo) nor "that of a water" (quel d'un'acqua) generates a penitential longing in Dante, making him lean and gaunt like his friend Forese. However, elsewhere, the pilgrim undergoes the same punishments as the souls in the *Purgatorio,* for example, passing through the wall of fire:

> When I was in, I would have plunged into boiling glass to cool off, so extreme was the burning.

> (Sì com fui dentro, in un bogliente vetro
> gittato mi sarei per rinfrescarmi,
> tant'era ivi lo 'ncendio sanza metro.)
> (*Purgatorio,* XXVII, 49–51)

Such narrative "variation" (variatio), however, has exclusively poetic or structural effects, since the operation of his personal ascetics is complete in both cases; just as in the *Inferno,* the type of individual divine judgment affirms disgust for sin whether simply by sight or by the test of experience—"Then I stretched out my hand/and plucked a small branch from a great thorn tree" (Allor porsi la mano un poco avante/ e colsi un ramicel da un gran pruno)—or even by subjective suffering—"and I was shivering in the eternal chill" (e io tremavo ne l'etterno rezzo).

In any case, the fiction of the narrative creates fewer important psychological inconsistencies in the ascetic field than in the mystical, precisely because Dante, who is not a mystic, must pretend to be one, while the ascetic experience is totally real and efficient with regard to those same sins or aspects of virtue whose examples, but not forms, are invented (Ciacco or Sapia, Brunetto or Forese). Within these very ample boundaries, Dante explores the rich casuistry in the texts of thirteenth-century asceticism, but fundamentally, he knows the moral truth of the many human adventures that he presents to us.

Precisely by virtue of this concreteness of personal experience, the *Commedia* is among the most accurate and profound repertories of ascetic examples in the history of Christian spirituality. Inquiries—which all of us are accustomed to make—into the sources of Dante's descriptions of scenes of damnation and penitence are deemphasized in the light of such an intense truth. Even these sources can be traced in part to the ascetic literature of the latter half of the thirteenth century, more to legendary saintly literature than to allegorical-didactic poems—the pains of hell, temptations of the devil, flames of purgatory, and beatitudes of paradise in the *Legenda aurea* and the *Actus beati Francisci,* in the legend of Margherita da Cortona, in the summaries of the lives of the Fathers in the Desert, in the temptations of Friar Egidio found in the additional chapters of the compilation *Actus-Fioretti,* in the legend of Blessed Umiliana de' Cerchi, and in various other thirteenth-century Dominican and Franciscan works.[9]

However, an investigation of the genre would be concerned more with Dante's literary preparation than with his ascetic commitment; I have tried to keep my remarks within the limits of the latter, which we must

9. For the *Vita Nuova,* see the rich series of affinities with Franciscan texts documented by V. Branca, "Poetica del rinnovamento e tradizione agiografica nella *Vita Nuova,*" in *Studi in onore di Italo Siciliano* (Firenze, Olschki, 1966).

see as the result of a quite subjective condition of soul, related to exigencies and concerns about which Dante only rarely gives us an explicit report (for example, the cord in *Inferno,* XVI, or the "fear" [paura] of the "torment from beneath" [tormento di sotto]; the "pride" [superbia] of *Purgatorio,* XIII; and elsewhere), but which he has established as a moral, sincere, and omnipresent condition.

4.

Dante's Idea of Love

BY THE REVEREND KENELM FOSTER, O.P.

Lecturer in Italian,
Cambridge University

It hardly needs to be said that love is a major theme
in Dante's work; enough to recall the figure of Beatrice
or indeed the concluding line of the *Comedy,* which
I propose to take as my own starting point: L'amor che
move il sole e l'altre stelle. It is a superb line, but it
raises questions. Just what does the poet mean by saying that love moves the world? What has this love-
impulse from God (for obviously "amor" here means
God) to do with the doctrine of creation? Why should
the conclusion of such a religious poem as this lay that
final stress on the physical world? Again, it may seem
at first sight odd that the climax of an ascent of the
human spirit to God should be expressed in terms of
two parallel impulses from God, the one driving
the sun and the stars, the other impelling a man's
desire and will: ma già volgeva il mio disio e il velle.

How, in short, is the concluding tercet of the *Paradiso* really conclusive?

From each of these questions others branch out, leading in all directions through the poet's work and into the culture that nourished it. Some points are clear from the start, however. It is clear that since love, for Dante, is an attribute of God, its presence in the created world is in some sense secondary and derived. But it is also clear from the whole context that the order and "rightness" of this world consist of a certain conformity to the divine love—a conformity which is given as *already* realized in the physical world, its actual present achievement being in the human spirit alone: the God-swayed motion of the stars is an objective fact to which a *newly* achieved state of one human soul is now being likened. Yet if we turn from the last canto of *Paradiso* to the first, it is clear that the relation between the physical and spiritual orders of creation is by no means only one of likeness; it is also, and first, one of coexistence as parts in a whole—the whole described by Beatrice in Canto I as that total order which forms the universe into a "likeness" of God:

> All things hold together in order, and it is this that makes the universe a likeness of God. It is here that the higher creatures see the trace of that eternal Goodness, which is the end for which that order was created.

> (Le cose tutte quante
> hanno ordine tra loro, e questo è forma
> che l'universo a Dio fa simigliante.
> Qui veggion l'alte creature l'orma

de l'etterno valore, il quale è fine
al quale è fatta la toccata norma.)
(*Paradiso*, I, 103–08)

The idea that God's likeness in the cosmos is the interrelated order of its parts can only be understood, as we
shall see later, in terms of a relation, expounded by
Dante in his prose *Convivio*, between the love-urge
in creatures and the original divine unity. However, it
is enough for the moment to note that the last tercet
and the first canto of *Paradiso* agree that the physical
and spiritual worlds form a single whole because they
both find their common measure in God—the etterno
valore of I, 107, the amor of XXXIII, 145.

A difference worth observing appears in the way
these distinct levels of reality are poetically represented.
At the close of Canto XXXIII the ultimate measuring
of creatures by God is stated with a stress on their passivity; the poet's will is impelled by the love which
also turns the stars in their courses. Now the expressive
aptness of this stress here, at the climax of the poem,
surely consists in its following immediately on Dante's
final statement of incapacity in the face of the over-
whelming Object he is encountering: "A l'alta fantasia
qui mancò possa; ma già volgeva" (*Paradiso*, XXXIII,
142–43). His spirit is now, in fact, beyond all the
physical heavens and all secondary causes; it has
reached the point of immediate contact with its Creator. This point is strictly ineffable, and this is just what
Dante, consciously or not, contrives to suggest by re-
lapsing from the spiritual to the physical, from the
unseen to the seen—expressing that mysterious point

67

of arrival in terms of the visible motion of the sun and stars. This at the same time serves to bring out a passivity that the situation must entail, for bodies— even heavenly ones—contrast with persons as being moved, not self-moving; as being more passive. The wheel image, introduced at this point, accentuates the note of passivity with the metrical stress falling on the passive participle: sí come rota ch'igualmente è mossa. The poet's spirit moves as a wheel is moved, as all the wheeling heavens are moved, by a force outside itself. However, this sort of "reduction" of spiritual state to physical movement, so apt at the *Paradiso's* close, would be out of place at its beginning; in fact, Beatrice's discourse on the dynamic order of the cosmos, while starting by placing all this under an original and continuing impetus from God, goes on to speak of creatures taking their own directions within the total system, each intrinsically impelled toward the divine Goodness—l'etterno valore, il qual è fine—and each therefore tending to its own distinctive approximation to the Goodness—più al principio loro e men vicine. Far from assimilating these various movements to a single "type," Beatrice is at pains to differentiate them in terms of degrees of affinity to the Creator:

> Thus things move to diverse harbors over the great sea of being and each with an impulse given it that bears it along.

> (onde si muovono a diversi porti
>   per lo gran mar dell'essere, e ciascuna
>   con istinto a lei dato che la porti.)
>   (*Paradiso,* I, 112–14)

Thus, the generalized "istinto" becomes, in creatures "c'hanno intelletto ed amore" (angels and men), a conscious attraction toward that light which is also perfect joy and is identified with the "happy target" of the Empyrean heaven, beyond all the physical "cieli," where Dante and his guide are now voyaging:

> and thither now, as to a place predetermined, we are being carried by the force of that bow-string which aims at a happy target whatever it lets fly.

> (e ora lí, come a sito decreto,
>   cen porta la vertú di quella corda
>   che ciò che scocca drizza in segno lieto.)
>   (*Paradiso*, I, 124–26)

In short, a main effect of this opening passage is to prepare for the description, which in fact will occupy the rest of the poem, of a particular kind of movement, a special kind of desire. It is Dante's thought on this desire, the kind that characterizes intelligent beings, that we must now try to elucidate.

The task is not easy, for it involves Dante's whole philosophy of man; indeed, one may say that all his thinking was, in one way or another, a reflection on love. For Dante, as for St. Augustine and Freud, this was the absolutely central topic. At the heart of his thought—and of his poetry—was a conception of the human soul as essentially attracted by things, as appetitive. It is surely no accident that the numerically central cantos of the *Comedy* (*Purgatorio* XVII–XVIII) are filled with Virgil's discourses on love; nothing Dante ever wrote is more characteristic, in respect to content, than two tercets from them, the first declaring the absolute universality of love, the second describing its emergence in the soul of man. I need hardly remind you of the former:

> "Neither Creator, my son, nor creature," he began, "was ever without love, whether natural or rational; and this you know."

> ("Né creator né creatura mai,"
> cominciò el, "figliuol, fu sanza amore,
> o naturale o d'animo; e tu 'l sai.")
> (*Purgatorio,* XVII, 91–93)

Do not be deceived by the quietness and relative abstractness of these lines. The tone is quiet because Dante's aim here is persuasion, and he must weigh every word. He is about to occupy himself with a vitally important doctrinal issue, the relation between the naturalness of love—declared in such unqualified terms a few moments before (Né creator né creatura mai . . .)—and moral responsibility. He is broaching his theory of free will, on which, as he well knows, the entire structure of his *Comedy* rests; and though I will return to this topic later, we shall not waste time if we reflect a little on his procedure at this point. It is characteristically dialectical and starts by presenting free will as apparently incompatible with the universality of the love-principle: every movement of the soul originates in a love of some kind, and love is always actually roused by something in the external world. The objection is stated as follows:

if love be offered us from outside us, and if the soul move in no other way, then it is not responsible for moving well or ill.

> (s'amore è di fuori a noi offerto,
>   e l'anima non va con altro piede,
>   se dritta o torta va, non è suo merto.)
>   (*Purgatorio,* XVIII, 43–45)

The answer—Virgil's and Dante's—is in effect to present free will as resulting from a difference between the rational soul's inborn and necessary drive toward self-fulfillment and an attraction to particular objects met in experience. Free will is the dialectical, self-critical relation within the living soul between itself as *simply* loving and itself as loving (or not) a particular thing. Thus the moral life appears as a constant measuring of particular attractions or repulsions against a single deeper attraction. However, the crucial point is the reality and nature of this deeper attraction. As an Aristotelian (more or less), Dante indeed stresses the passive element in experience: all knowledge starts in sensation, and so too every actual desire. The love-capacity must always, in the concrete, be roused by an external object:

> Your apprehensive power, having drawn an impression from some existing thing, unfolds it within you, so that this turns the mind to itself; and if, thus turned, you lean towards it, that leaning is love.

> (Vostra apprensiva da esser verace
>   tragge intenzione, e dentro a voi la spiega

sí che l'animo ad essa volger face;
e se, rivolto, inver di lei si piega,
   quel piegare è amor.)
           (*Purgatorio,* XVIII, 22–26)

However, to save free will he was obliged to find an interior psychic principle to offset this passivity to external things—a principle by which to measure external things with respect to desirability and value and which would be the determining factor in actually choosing between them. This principle Dante found, as was to be expected, in the mind or reason, and he traced its determining power in the act of choice back to the mind's being a direct effect (sanza mezzo) of the Creator. But to say this is to anticipate; in the *Purgatorio* cantos we are at present considering any special relation of the rational soul to God is only implicit. What these cantos do make clear, and what is relevant to our inquiry, may be summarized as follows. All human activity springs, directly or indirectly, from love of some kind. When our conscious life begins, we find ourselves already inclined toward certain primary objects of desire (i primi appetibili), and this inclination, since it precedes any and every act of choice, is not under our control. This same original inclination continues throughout life as a primary desire (prima voglia), which nevertheless we *are* able to control, insofar as, before consenting to it, we pass it through our inborn power of reflection and deliberation:

> inborn in you is the power that deliberates, and
> that should guard the threshold of assent.

(innata v'è la virtù che consiglia
e de l'assenso de' tener la soglia).
(*Purgatorio,* XVIII, 62–63)

Finally, we can infer from Dante's statements here,
though he does not make the point explicitly, that the
object of the primary desire is radically one, not many,
for though this desire is explicitly said to bear on certain primi appetibili, the context allows us to identify
it with *one* radical desire for happiness or self-fulfillment. This point will, I hope, become clear from
what must now be said of the measuring or normative
function in the moral life of that primary desire.

This desire as such does not deliberate, but the
moral life only begins when deliberation (la virtù che
consiglia) comes into play. This deliberative "virtù" or
power pertains of course to reason or intellect, and
elsewhere, when speaking of free will, Dante will
stress the intellectual factor in it. However, in such
cases he is either defining free will or declaring its relative independence of physical environment;[1] here, in
Purgatorio XVIII, his concern is to show free choice
as an activity integral to the very process of human
desire itself, as a factor emerging quite spontaneously
in and from the pursuit of happiness and which gives
to this pursuit all its moral quality, as being, in a given
case, ethically either right or wrong. In short, the stress
here is on the moral implications of free will and,
consequently, on its appetitive and volitional rather

1. As in *Monarchia,* I, xii, 1–6, or *Purgatorio,* XVI,
67–81.

than its rational-cognitive aspect. It seems to me what is most original in Dante's thought at this point is his presenting the primary desire as precisely the ultimate interior "measure," which not only, together with rational deliberation, makes free choice possible but also provides free choice with its moral norm or rule. The norm of morality, as Dante presents it here, is not sufficiently described as right reason, nor is it, directly, God, nor, much less, any abstract idea of duty; it is first and foremost the living human soul itself in its inborn and essential craving for happiness; and this because that craving can only in fact be fulfilled by God. Nothing less than this fulfillment is implied in man's "confused" natural desire for happiness.[2] Such will be the explicit lesson of the *Paradiso,* but it is already implied here in Virgil's affirmation of the inviolable authority, the sacredness, as we may call it, of the primary desire, of that deepest human inclination which is the proper rule and measure of man's life on earth:

> Now in order that every other desire be gathered in to this one, inborn in you is the power that deliberates, and that should hold the threshold of assent.

> (or perché a questa ogn' altra si raccoglia
> innata v'è la virtù che consiglia,
> e de l'assenso de' tener la soglia.)
> (*Purgatorio,* XVIII, 61–63)

The verb "si raccoglia" I render literally—"be gathered in"—and I take this metaphor to signify that the

2. Cf. *Purgatorio,* XVII, 127–29.

moral acceptability of each particular desire is judged in relation to the primary one: it is morally good only so far as it subserves the latter. The primary desire, then, is in this sense normative and supreme. However, as a rule for conduct it takes effect, of course, only through deliberation, so that we may conclude that the whole purpose of deliberation (consiglio) is to mediate between the basic primary desire, whose rightness is not in question, and all the other, particular desires, whose rightness is very much in question.

Observe, however, that this rightness of the primary desire, though it underpins morality, is not in itself ethical, for it does not follow free choice, it precedes it; it is in no way the product of free will, and as such it cannot bring praise or blame—merto di lode o di biasmo non cape (*Purgatorio,* XVIII, 60). What one can be praised for is any choice in conformity with it; what one can be blamed for is any other choice. Let us call its rightness ontological. It has to do with what man *is* prior to anything he deliberately does; with his nature rather than with what he does with it; with man as God's product, not his own. As Dante sees it, the rightness at the root of our nature is simply the effect of the divine Goodness which created it.

Before pursuing this last, and very important point, let us step back a little and view things in a wider historical perspective. Dante's general theory of love falls easily into place as a variant on the Platonic tradition. Plato had taught that human love (eros) could, properly trained, become a love of ideal goodness and beauty. The later Platonists, especially Plotinus, de-

veloped their master's teaching by combining his notion of the absolute divine Good with his ideas about
human eros.[3] Thus Plotinus conceived of the Deity, the
One or Good, not only as the universal source of goodness but also—and this point is crucial—as the source
of eros itself, of an aspiration in all things toward the
absolute Goodness: He gives "a dynamic being which
turns back towards its source, which looks, tends,
strives towards Him: and in us this movement back to
our source is *eros,* a love given by and conforming us
to the Good we love."[4] "The soul," says Plotinus,
"loves Him (God), moved by Him to love from the
beginning."[5] Moreover God, as the active source of
eros, may be called not only *erasmion* (lovable) but
eros (love itself): "He is at once lovable, and love, and
love of Himself."[6] Thus, in Aristotelian terms, the
ultimate final cause of eros has become its ultimate
efficient cause as well; the upward path from the many
to the One, from creatures to God, implies a prior
downward path. Eros moves in a circle; things return
through it to God because they came through it from
God. It only remained for Proclus to draw out more
clearly the affinity between the One and the many that
the system involved. Whatever proceeds from the
One is, in one sense, the same as it, in another sense,
different. As the same, it can be said to "remain" in
its source; it differs only as "proceeding" from it. But

3. See A. H. Armstrong, "Platonic *Eros* and Christian
Agape," *Downside Review,* 79 (1961), 105–21.
4. Ibid., p. 113.
5. *Enneads,* VI, 7, 31; 9, 9.
6. Ibid., VI, 8, 15. See J. M. Rist, *Eros and Psyche*
(Toronto, Toronto University Press, 1964), pp. 78–112.

the remaining (μονή) takes effect dynamically as a natural tendency in each thing to complete the movement of proceeding (πρόοδος) by one of "turning back" (επιστροφή).[7] The whole cosmos follows this triadic pattern, whose unifying principle is eros.

A fairly direct line leads from this Neoplatonism to Dante, even though it lies through Christianity. The religion of the Bible had had, and would continue to have, difficulties with Neoplatonism, but not with respect to the basic triadic pattern of procession and return through love. The points of difference concerned, not the reality of such a cyclic movement, but how it took effect. For Christians the *proodos* from God entailed creation in the strict sense, a non-necessary causing of being *ex nihilo,* an idea alien to the Greek mind. The *epistrophe* to God entailed Christ, the incarnate Redeemer, a "folly to the Greeks." Nevertheless, love was for Christianity also—indeed, more emphatically —the principle of both *proodos* and *epistrophe.* In this respect the tradition of eros was congenial to Christian theology. It could, of course, reappear therein in ways that were more or less authentically Christian, but differences of this kind need not concern us here. The question whether Dante was at all points an orthodox Catholic is a real question, but the scope of my paper does not include it. The essential features of his love-doctrine are historically explained by Neoplatonist influences, but in themselves they do not imply any weakening of Christian dogma, any more than similar influences did in the case of William of St. Thierry or St. Thomas Aquinas, both of whom took much from

7. Proclus, *Elements of Theology,* Prop. 30–35.

Denys. What they—and, in general, the Christian thinkers of the high Middle Ages—took from Neoplatonist tradition, as filtered through this respected Dionysian medium, especially concerned two vital points in Catholic theology, each connected with a key text of Scripture—the identification of God with Love (*Deus caritas est,* I John 4:16) and the identification of man with God's image (*Et creavit Deus hominem ad imaginem suam; ad imaginem Dei creavit illum,* Gen. 1:27). Not only were both doctrines easily to be found in Denys' *Divine Names* but also the eros link between them.[8] God is eros and the cause of eros —which, in St. Thomas' scholastic language, becomes, "God is love both *essentialiter et causaliter.*" God has the fullness of being, which is goodness, and this He loves; and since all that is in Him is simply Himself, then He is the love whereby He loves Himself.[9] Therefore whatever God makes will be a created image of absolute love, and as such a lover of absolute goodness. From this point of view, then, it means exactly the same to say, "I am created" and "I am a lover of God"; to say, "I have come from God" (by *proodos*) and "I am returning to God" (by *epistrophe*). To discover oneself as a creature is to discover oneself desiring one's Creator, and vice versa. With this we are already back in Dante's company, though certain special Dantean themes and insights have yet to be touched on. But the general pattern is emerging. When

8. Cf. St. Thomas, *Expositio super Dionysium, De Divinis Nominibus,* Chap. 4, lectio xi passim, ed. Mandonnet (Paris, 1927), pp. 399–403.
9. Ibid., pp. 400–01.

in the *Convivio* Dante declares that "the chief desire in everything, and the first given it by nature, is to return to Him" (*IV*, xii, 14), he refers explicitly to the Genesis text on the Image, but there can be no doubt that he also had in mind the Neoplatonist *Liber de Causis*, cited earlier in a very similar context, and perhaps even Denys' *Divine Names* and St. Thomas' commentary on it. The pattern, in any case, is the same circular one that St. Thomas, in this work, explicitly mentions: *quaedam enim circulatio apparet in amore, secundum quod est ex bono et ad bonum*—though shifting the emphasis slightly from *amor* to its concomitant *bonum;* for the goodness of God is the precise and proper reason for both His loving Himself and His consequent outpouring into creatures, which of their nature must love Him in return: *ex isto bono (Deus) emanavit in existentia, et iterum in existentibus participatus convertit se ad suum principuum, quod est bonum.*[10]

You may be wondering by now when I am going to mention a woman other than the lady of the *Divine Comedy*. But this is a study of Dante's ideas on love, not an essay in biography; and the feminine figures that appear in Dante's lyric verse—Violetta, the Pargoletta, the Pietra lady, Beatrice herself under this aspect—can only concern us as occasions arousing the poet to theorize about love; and little can be said here even about such theorizing in the lyrics, with the *Comedy* always pressing for attention. Yet it must of course be emphasized that long before Dante set his

10. Ibid., p. 403.

hand to the "sacred poem" he was a poet of "profane" love, and that one very erotic canzone may well have been written after the *Comedy* was begun.[11]

What does all this lyric poetry—in which I include the *Vita Nuova*—tell us that is relevant to our theme? One fact is clear—this love poetry has nothing to do with marriage. This will surprise only those unacquainted with medieval literature. Though there is no evidence that Dante ever subscribed to the extreme view held by Andreas Capellanus in his celebrated *De Amore* (late twelfth century) that true love was essentially an extramarital relation,[12] Dante never shows—not even in the *Comedy*—any special interest in married love. Apart from a few allusions to the wrongness of adultery and a few hints in praise of happy family life, he ignores the subject. It is one of his most interesting differences from Milton.

Yet if sexual love is not by Dante explicitly related —or only in passing and marginally—to Christian marriage, he was, of course, a Christian—passionately so in later life, to judge from the *Comedy,* and conventionally so, at least, in youth, to judge from the *Vita Nuova.* So the question arises, how did Dante relate sexual love to his religion? This is a complex question, involving far more than the individual Dante's attitudes; and here I can do no more than indicate certain salient points that need, I think, to be borne in mind in approaching it. But first one general observation—Dante's metaphysics, so to call it, of

11. *Amor, da che convien* (*Rime* CXVI). Its probable date is 1307–08.

12. Andreas Capellanus, *De Amore,* Chap. 6, ed. Trojel (Copenhagen, 1892), pp. 150–55.

sexuality is far more positive and optimistic than his view of its actual effects in human life. Abstractly considered, sexuality is thoroughly good; in the concrete, in its practical effects, it is often evil—damnably so. This, generally speaking, is the outlook of the *Comedy,* the work in which Dante records and takes stock of all his manifold experience of human life in the light of the Christian faith.

Thus, given the nature and scope of the poem, it is inevitable that whatever is said about love in it should be, at least implicitly and indirectly, critical and self-critical. The "Dante-personage" who makes that journey through the afterlife is a sinner when he begins it, and the whole point of the journey, as the poem itself declares, is to effect a conversion in the will— his own will first and then his readers'—from sin to God.[13] The means to this end is a growth in knowledge of the nature of good and evil; hence, the *Inferno* gives knowledge of evil, and the other two *cantiche* give knowledge of good. All this, in one way or another, is a study of love. Metaphysically it had to be so for Dante, as we have seen; and introspection showed that it was so, that all our actions, good or bad, implied a love of some kind:

> . . . love must be the seed in you of every virtue
> and of every deed deserving punishment.

> (ch'esser convene
> amor sementa in voi d'ogni virtute,
> e d'ogne operazion che merta pene.)

> (*Purgatorio,* XVII, 103–05)

13. See esp. *Purgatorio,* XXX, 127–41; XXXII, 103–05; XXXIII, 52–54.

Amor here is *eros* in the wide trans-sexual sense already noted—St. Thomas' *amor naturalis*.[14] But as Virgil's discourse continues into the argument about free will, a specific sexual reference becomes discernible; this is natural enough, given that Dante had been a man of the world before he became a theologian, and a poet of profane love before he set out to sublimate *amor* into *caritas.*

Now, profane love had then its own type or types of sublimation in the courtly love tradition which Dante imbibed in his teens and which, though he later became its critic, he never repudiated. Courtly love is a large subject, and if I venture in passing, in connection with the sublimations it involved, to refer to Cicero's *De Amicitia,* it is not that I have a formed opinion as to the direct influence of that work on the twelfth-century troubadours (though certainly it was influential at that time and notably with the chief theorist of courtly love, Andreas Capellanus), but that Cicero's ideal of disinterested affection seems to offer an illuminating parallel, one valid undoubtedly for the *Vita Nuova.* Is it an oversimplification to see *fin amors* as a transposition into a heterosexual context of Cicero's ideal of a love that would have no end outside itself (*omnis eius fructus in ipso amore est*)?[15] The heterosexual context implied an element of desire that is absent in Cicero—what is more, desire intensely cultivated. But the main object of this cultivation, at least

14. *Summa Theologica,* 1a 2ae, 26. 1; cf 1a. 20. 1.
15. Cicero, *De Amicitia,* IX, 31.

ostensibly, was much the same as that of Ciceronian friendship—the moral perfection of the lover. It was generally assumed by the love-poets and emphatically taught by Capellanus that love was the chief source of moral goodness and, consequently, that to be a true lover was to be committed to virtuous living, even if the virtues entailed would not get full marks from the Church.

However, this ethical stress toward sublimation is less important, in Dante's writings, than the connected but logically distinct idea of natural nobility. Everything, Dante declares, is "noble" in the degree that its distinctive nature is realized; not only a man but also a stone or a tree or a horse or a hawk is noble insofar as it perfectly realizes its nature. Human nature is the rational soul informing appropriate matter. Whenever these two principles are fitly and harmoniously interrelated you have a noble man or woman—the innate quality of "gentilezza" (*Convivio,* IV, xvi). This gentilezza is not precisely a moral quality, since, like the prima voglia discussed above, it pertains to the nature one originally receives prior to any act of the will. It is not virtue, though without virtue it remains more or less latent and inoperative. As a man or woman grows up, it shows itself first in the emotions and then, if virtue supervenes, in the reason and will. Sexual attraction then, as part of human nature, is naturally noble; and Dante, as an heir of the courtly love tradition, was disposed from the start to see in a person's susceptibility to it a very clear sign of innate gentilezza, indeed to see the two as virtually inseparable. "Amore e il cor gentil

83

sono una cosa," he declares in the *Vita Nuova,* echoing his revered master Guinizelli's famous line, "Al cor gentil rempaira sempre amore."

But it was in the *Convivio,* written in middle age, that Dante worked out his theory of human gentilezza with a brilliant application of the Aristotelian concepts of matter and form. The historical importance of this development consists chiefly, I suggest, in that the long analysis of gentilezza in *Convivio* IV gave for the first time to the literary and vaguely erotic notion of *cor gentile* a central place in a philosophical treatise *de homine.* Extending the meaning of this term outside its usual erotic context, Dante made it a basic element in a new humanism.

In calling Dante's humanism new I do not mean that the idea of man we find in the *Convivio* is radically novel. It is still, basically, the idea worked out by the Christian fathers and scholastics using the double source material of Scripture and Greek philosophy. The novelty lies in the fact that this material is now rethought by a layman writing for laymen and, more important, by a poet nourished on a literary tradition which, while it had already been affected by philosophy, had hitherto had only very tenuous connections with theology. Dante's own interest in Christian theology appears only marginally in the *Convivio,* for this book, while obviously the work of a Christian, celebrates the discoveries of reason far more than the mysteries of faith. Nevertheless, it is in places where the argument of the treatise touches, or approaches, theology that Dante develops his ideas on love in the most interesting way. The passages I have in mind deal, respectively, with love as a "cosmic principle" deriving from the nature of God (*Convivio,* III, ii); with the influence of the heaven of Venus (II, v); and with the love-capacity in man as a constituent of his specific nobility and as a tending of its nature (though, as we shall see, the tendency can well be thwarted) to the fulfillment of the specific human possibilities—that is, to a perfection proper to man as man in this life, consisting in knowledge and virtue, and to a higher perfection reserved for the next life, consisting in the vision of God (III, ii; IV, xxii, cf. xii). I will mainly confine myself in what follows to the first and second of these points, though what I shall say will also, I hope, throw some light on the third one, which in any case has already been touched on in connection with the "primary desire." This will conclude what I shall say about the ideal scope and development of human love as Dante saw it, leaving for a brief final consideration his teaching on the corruption that commonly mars and distorts it.

We have already seen, from the *Paradiso,* how Dante relates love to God through the moving order of the cosmos: all movement in creation is an effect of God's love, and the resulting order is God's "likeness" in the universe. The reasoning implicit here seems to run as follows: effects represent or resemble their causes; God's effects resemble Him in the degree that they are perfect; a whole is more perfect than its parts; therefore, the whole universe resembles God more than any part of it. But this does not yet render all Dante's thought; it leaves out the dynamic element of movement, in particular that "spiritual movement" (moto spiritale) which is the love-desire of intelligent creatures (*Purgatorio*, XVIII, 32). So it seems that a rider must be added: the love-desire of intelligent creatures gets the perfection that makes it "resemble" God precisely through its relation to the universe as a whole. Just such a relation is what we find sketched out in a prose passage of exceptional philosophical interest in *Convivio*, III, ii, 2–9, which in turn presupposes the last two chapters of Book I. All love (we read in the latter text) is an attraction to some goodness in an object and is intense in proportion to the nearness of that object. But to a sentient or intelligent being things become near through being known; hence, *ceteris paribus* the more knowledge the more love. Now love itself, Virgil told us on Mount Purgatory, passes through three stages: first, apprehension of something as desirable; second, desire of it (moto spiritale); third, possession and enjoyment of it—the soul, once desire has set it moving, being unable to rest, "until the thing loved brings it joy" (fin che la cosa amata il fa gioire) (*Purgatorio*, XVIII, 33). It is however with this third and final stage that Dante, in *Convivio*, III, ii, 3, identifies love in general, defining this as the union to which desire tends ("unimento spirituale de l'anima e de la cosa amata"), "toward which union," he adds, "the soul runs of its own nature, and swiftly or slowly according as it is free or hindered." Why "of its own nature"? Because, quite simply, this nature comes from God. God is the primal unity from which all the diversity of creation proceeds. Each creature has, then, a natural affinity to unity—hence, the relevance of the expression "unimento spirituale." Moreover, in God, unity and being are one, and with a union that is precisely a loving. Therefore the soul has also a natural affinity to being and so a natural and necessary love of being. Since God is the cause of its being, the soul's very nature draws it toward God, in order to maintain and strengthen itself in being. Thus of necessity our soul desires the primal Goodness which is God, and this desire is basic and primary. It is only in *consequence* that we cleave to created things, inasmuch as it is through them the divine Goodness "shows" itself. This is to say that man's appetite for God has to take effect through a knowledge of God that is necessarily indirect, since human intelligence is only brought into play by sense experience. Thus our relationship to God appears differently according to the appetitive or the cognitive sides of our nature. As appetitive we are attached to God *directly* and from the first moment of existence; as cognitive we have to approach Him *indirectly* through the medium of experience and concepts—through those "showings" of God which are the "goodnesses" ("le bontadi") that the mind apprehends in Nature or in itself. From this point of view the soul's approach to God will be a uniting of itself spiritually (unimento spirituale) with the rest of the universe and thus the constituting of an intellectual "order" analogous to that total "ordine" which is creation's likeness to the Creator according to *Paradiso*, I (*Convivio*, III, ii, 2–9).[16]

So far we are in the realm of metaphysics, the pattern of ideas we have been tracing being clearly a

16. Cf. *Convivio*, III, iv, 9; *Paradiso*, IV, 40–42.

variant on the Neoplatonist tradition that all things go in a cyclic movement from and to the divine One or Good. We must now touch briefly on the important part played in this cyclic movement, as Dante saw it, by influences descending from the physical heavens, the stars and planets. It is certain that Dante believed in such influences and thought that human life—to say nothing of plants and animals—was deeply affected by them. An individual had certain propensities—aggressive, studious, amative, etc.—because he was born under a certain star or constellation; moreover a man born under one influence might also in time come under another. Dante himself was born under the Twins, and he owed much to them, but he also acknowledges emphatically the influence of Venus, the star of love: "lo bel pianeta che d'amar conforta" (*Purgatorio*, I, 19).[17] The implications of this view of things in his thought about man are complex and far-reaching; for our purpose it is enough to note three points in particular.

First, Dante insists strongly—and even more in the *Convivio* than in the *Comedy*—that in this process of "influencing" the physical heavens act only as instruments. The chief agents are the great intelligences that move them, "whom the common folk call angels" (*Convivio*, II, iv, 2),[18] these of course being good

17. Cf. *Paradiso*, XX, 112–20.
18. The sketch that follows of the role of the angels in transmitting influences through the stars and planets is based chiefly on *Convivio*, II, iv–v; *Paradiso*, II, 127–44; VII, 130–41; VIII, 97–148; XIII, 52–78; XXVIII, 64–78.

angels, not bad ones or devils. Dante's universe is entirely controlled by good powers. Moreover, these powers are all in direct contact with God and from Him draw the "virtue" which they then pour downward through the heavens. This clearly is the case with all the astral influences and is explicitly stated regarding the influence from Venus, "by which souls (anime) here below are enkindled to love, according to their disposition" (*Convivio,* II, v, 13). Indeed, Dante goes further than this; he makes the influence of Venus derive precisely from the Third Person of the Christian Trinity, the Holy Spirit, inasmuch as the angelic order appointed to move the heaven of Venus has for its special object of contemplation "the supreme and most fervent love of the Holy Spirit" (*Convivio,* II, v, 8). Since the term "souls" (anime) in the phrase quoted above certainly refers to principles of physical life—and not only in man but also in lower animals and plants—it is clear that Dante is relating sexual attraction in general to the Holy Spirit by way of the Venus-heaven and its angel-movers. He could hardly have expressed more clearly his sense of the interpenetration of spirit and matter in the universe and of the natural "holiness" of every manifestation of love. It is against this background that we should understand those otherwise surprisingly erotic declarations of Cunizza da Romano and Folco of Marseilles in *Paradiso* IX. Both of these blessed souls, now appearing to the poet in Venus, had been overcome on earth by the "light" of the star of love, and both now rejoice in the fact—not in the sin that this occasioned, but in the amative influence itself, which (it is implied) they were able, through repentance, to turn to good effect:

> Here we do not repent—we smile; not at the sin, which does not come to mind any more, but at the Goodness which ordered and foresaw.

> (non de la colpa, ch'a mente non torna,
> ma del valor ch'ordinò e provide.)
>
> (*Paradiso,* IX, 103–05)[19]

Sexual attraction, like everything else, falls within God's providence and can and should find its issue in love for God. Perhaps, too, the poet is here implicitly justifying the role of Beatrice in his *Comedy.*

And this dependence of astral influences, through the angels, on the Trinity had, I think, another important implication for Dante—one that he never expounds systematically, but that he twice hints at in the *Paradiso* (IV, 55–63; VIII, 1–9). It has to do with his interpretation of pagan religion, as known to him through the Latin classics. This topic deserves a lecture itself; here I can only touch on it so far as my theme requires.[20] Briefly, Dante saw the polytheism of the gentili as due to a mistake about natural forces arising from ignorance about the angels, from the "difetto d'ammaestramento," the lack of divine teaching that obtained in the world, outside the chosen people, before the coming of Christ. The pagans—the ordinary folk, not the philosophers—were vaguely aware of influences and powers in the heavens, but in

19. Cf. *Paradiso,* IX, 32–36.
20. On this matter see esp. P. Renucci, *Dante, Juge et disciple du monde gréco-romain* (Paris, 1954).

their ignorance of the angelic orders—controlling intelligences that were, nonetheless, absolutely creatures of the one true God—they divinized those heavenly forces:

> This principle [the fact of star influence], misunderstood, formerly led almost all the world astray, so that it ran off calling on the names of Jove and Mercury and Mars.

> (Questo principio male inteso, torse
>   già tutto il mondo quasi, sì che Giove
>   Mercurio e Marte a nominar trascorse.)
> (*Paradiso*, IV, 61–63; *Convivio*, II, iv, 6–7)

It was both religious and moral error; with idolatry went immorality (for Dante as for St. Paul), and we can hardly be surprised that he pauses to stress this fact as he enters the heaven of Venus, of eros:

> The world used to believe, in its peril, that the fair Cyprian rayed down insane love, turning in the third epicycle; so that not only her did they honor with sacrifice and votive cry, those ancient people in their ancient error, but they honored Dione also and Cupid.

> (Solea creder lo mondo in suo periclo
>   che la bella Ciprigna il folle amore
>   raggiasse, volta nel terzo epiciclo;
> per che non pur a lei faceano onore
>   di sacrificio e di votivo grido
>   le genti antiche ne l'antico errore,
> ma Dione onoravano e Cupido.)
> (*Paradiso*, VIII, 1–7)

The belief that a love-influence came from the third heaven was not false; but it *was* a false step to derive precisely "folle amore," love as dethroning reason, from the heavens and a worse one to *divinize* the source of sin, to place a goddess in the love-star, the "fair Cyprian"—a product of man's erring imagination—in a place that was rightly due to angels of God. This error we can, quite clearly, see Dante correcting, as the two Venus cantos continue, with allusions to the angelic hierarchy to which the souls appearing in this planet, and so the planet itself, are related, and to the Providence that governs the star influences generally (VIII, 34–37, 97 ss.; IX, 61–63, 76–78). It is in effect a Christian critique of paganism by "demythologizing." The veil of fable is removed; the goddess dethroned; and her planet, now seen in its true relation to the angels and their Creator, is at one stroke undivinized and yet the more ennobled.

This leads to my third point: the critique I speak of was a placing of the physical world in relation to not only superhuman spiritual powers but also, implicitly, to man's own spirit, in particular, to free will. The question of free will is prominent in the *Comedy*, chiefly for two historically connected reasons: first, the prevalence of theories of astral determinism, deriving largely from Arabic sources; second, the fact that in the *Comedy* Dante is reacting against a strain of fatalism in the current talk about sexual love, a fatalism he may well have thought he himself had encouraged in some of his lyrics. He confronts astral determinism as such directly in *Purgatorio* XVI, in Marco Lombardo's great assertion of the immediate dependence of the human mind of God, with the consequence that the mind is not, in principle, subject to the heavens:

> To a greater power [than that of the heavens] and a better nature you are subject in freedom; and it is this that creates mind in you, which is not in charge of the heavens.

> A maggior forza e a miglior natura
> liberi soggiacete; e quella cria
> la mente in voi, che 'l ciel non ha in sua cura.
>
> (*Purgatorio*, XVI, 79–81)

The other psychological fatalism, which saw free will as powerless against passion, had, on the whole, a more literary, less "scholastic" tradition behind it. Dante himself had superbly expressed it in some of his profane love poems, notably in the Montanina canzone and in a famous sonnet to Cino, "Io sono stato con Amore insieme"; and perhaps the best—certainly the briefest —way to bring his mature critique of this erotic fatalism to a sharp focus is to contrast the denial of free will contained in that sonnet with the assertion of it contained in the central discourse of *Purgatorio,* already in part analyzed. In effect, the latter text recants the former.

Stripped of its grand imagery, the gist of the sonnet is this: Having been familiar with love since boyhood, I know that reason and virtue are powerless against it; that within its sphere of influence free will is *not* free and all deliberation is useless:

> Therefore within the circle of his (love's) arena free will was never free, so that in vain is deliberation there shot forth.

93

(Però nel cerchio de la sua palestra
liber arbitrio già mai non fu franco,
sì che consiglio invan vi si balestra.)
(*Rime,* CXI, ll. 9–11)

Dante's friend Cino asked if he, having been one woman's lover, should yield to the love he had begun to feel for another. Dante's answer is "Yes, for love is irresistible." It is worth noting that in a prose letter accompanying his sonnet, Dante is equally affirmative but does not mention free will, basing his answer on the natural changeability of the concupiscible appetite, "the seat of love" (*Epistole,* III, 3). This love is of course carnal love, whose seat is the living animal body, which, as material, is subject to the physical heavens. Thus the phrase in the sonnet, "nel cerchio de la sua palestra," refers to this world as subject to influences from Venus. Human free will is in this world, and whether or not it is by nature subject to those influences (a point ignored in the sonnet), it cannot in fact resist them; the force of the lower appetites, aroused by those influences, is too strong. It is precisely this doctrine that the *Comedy* corrects—first, as we have seen in *Purgatorio* XVI, as regards the basic natural independence of free will vis-à-vis the heavens; second, in *Purgatorio* XVIII, as regards the ability of free will to resist passion. The wording of the latter correction, with the stress on the role of "consiglio" ("la virtù che consiglia"), strongly suggests that in writing it Dante had just that sonnet of his in mind. In any case, without this assertion of the power of free choice against the pull of sense appetite, his "sacred poem" would have lacked an essential doctrinal component. Hence, perhaps, the explicit association here of free will and Beatrice: "By this noble power Beatrice understands free will" (La nobile virtú Beatrice intende per lo libero arbitrio) (*Purgatorio,* XVIII, 73–74).

The allusion here is to Beatrice in her quasi-symbolic function as the voice of Christian wisdom, of *sacra doctrina,* so evident in the *Paradiso.* However, in the poem as a whole she is, of course, not only Dante's teacher about moral freedom (and other things). She actually gives him freedom ("Tu m'hai di servo tratto a libertate"—*Paradiso,* XXXI, 85); and we have already begun to see what she freed him from—subjection to the stars and errors about them, and his own carnal appetite. Let us note this connection of error, sensuality, and enslavement; the three themes are closely interwoven, and they come to a compelling focus in that female symbol which, of all the figures in the *Comedy,* stands most clearly in opposition to Beatrice—I mean the Siren who makes her appearance, significantly, in the canto immediately following the discourse on free will which ends on the name of her heavenly adversary. The Siren is born of sleep and dream ("mi venne in sogno") and born, at first, hideous; her rebirth into beauty is a purely psychic action proceeding from the dreamer himself. As Dante gazes at her, she is transformed by his gazing; and giving her beauty, he falls under a spell of his own making. Even the sweetness of her song comes from him, the song in which she exults over her prey:

"I am," she sang, "I am the sweet siren who leads
sailors astray in mid-sea, so delicious am I to hear!
. . . and he who stays with me seldom departs, so
entirely do I satisfy him!"

("Io son," cantava, "io son dolce serena
   che i marinari in mezzo mar dismago;
   tanto son di piacere a sentir piena!
   . . . e qual meco si ausa,
   rado sen parte; sí tutto l'appago!")
                    (*Purgatorio,* XIX, 7–24)

The whole stress then of this wonderful episode is on
the subjectivity of carnal sin and thus on the delusion
involved in that "twisted love" (l'amor torto) which,
in the canto on charity (*Paradiso* XXVI), will be directly contrasted with "straight love" (amor diritto)
(ll. 62–63); the metaphor implies of course that in
loving creatures to excess the soul deflects from the
path to God marked out by its nature—by that primary
drive toward God that the prima voglia, as we have
seen, implies. But note particularly the element of error
involved. For Dante (as for St. Thomas) all sin involves
an initial mistake. At its most venial, at a scarcely culpable stage at all, this mistake appears in the child's
turning and cleaving to "little goods" *as though they
were final,* as though, in fact, they were the uncreated
Good it already unconsciously desires:

    the utterly simple soul that knows nothing except
    that, come from the hands of a happy maker, she
    willingly turns to whatever gives her pleasure.
    First she tastes the savor of some little good; and

this beguiles her and after it she runs, if some
guide or curb do not turn her love aside.

> (l'anima semplicetta che sa nulla
>   salvo che, mossa da lieto fattore,
>   volentier torna a ciò che la trastulla.
> Di picciol bene in pria sente sapore;
>   quivi s'inganna, e dietro ad esso corre,
>   se guida o fren non torce suo amore.)
>   (*Purgatorio,* XVI, 88–93)

At a more conscious and culpable level the mistake
will be that of Francesca, deluded by her literary
romanticism—"Love, that is swiftly kindled in a noble
heart . . . Love, that allows no loved one not to love in
return" (Amor, ch'al cor gentil ratto s'apprende . . .
Amor, ch'a nullo amato amar perdona—*Inferno,* V,
100–03)—by the strain of illusion in courtly love of
which *Inferno* V is so telling and discreet a critique.
To understand the psychology implied in this critique
of an error that is of both mind and will, at once a
mistake and a moral fault, let us turn back again to
the prose *Convivio.* In Books I and III of this work a
series of texts relate error, both intellectual and moral,
to the difference between sense and reason and the
influence of passion. Man has both sense and reason,
but sensation comes first in time and in most men it
remains the dominant factor; they remain childish all
their lives, judging by outward appearances and as
their emotions are affected. The "eye of reason"—
which sees further and deeper than the senses, seeing
in things an intrinsic order of means to ends and so an
objective goodness and badness—remains dim in most

men; this is chiefly because subjective emotion confuses and distorts judgment. As emotion increases, so does the risk of misjudgment, and emotion grows as the object causing it (whether of attraction or repulsion) draws *near* the apprehending subject: "the more the agent unites with the patient, the more passion does the latter feel . . . hence the nearer the thing desired gets to the desirer, the more desire grows, and the soul, becoming more impassioned, ever more identifies itself with the sense appetite and ever more abandons reason." The result, in effect, is a lapse from the human to the animal level: "so that then the soul no longer judges humanly of a person (whom it apprehends), but in a more or less animal way, simply by outward appearances and with no discernment of truth" (*Convivio,* III, x, 2).[21]

The phrase, "non discernendo la veritade," on Dante's lips, is pregnant indeed, for truth is "the good of the intellect" and God is ultimate truth. To lose sight of truth is to begin to miss the way to God. It is also, as we have seen, a lapse from humanity, and the general cause of such a lapse is now clear enough too. It is that desire tends ever to outrun knowledge, the soul as appetitive being pulled irresistibly toward a final good which, as cognitive, it only vaguely apprehends, and the true identity of which, and the right means to which, it is ever in danger of misapprehending; this occurring precisely because of that initial imbalance in it of cognition and appetite. Since cognition begins in sensation, in the animal part of man,

21. Cf. *Convivio,* I, iv, 3; xi, 3.

the misjudgments due to the imbalance tend, as evaluations, to be subhuman, and this, as we have seen, involves both illusion and loss of freedom. For Dante, what particularly loses freedom in this process is the faculty of free will itself. It is the situation summarized toward the end of Book I of the *Monarchia:*

> Insofar as judgment entirely moves appetite . . . it is free; but insofar as appetite, taking the initiative in any way, moves the judgment, the latter cannot be free; for in this case it does not act of itself but is drawn to act as the captive of another. (xii, 3–4)

The usual Dantean name for this "other"—the force that outruns reason and drags it awry or downward—is cupidity (cupidigia, cupiditas), and the chief symbolic representations of it are the Siren and the She-Wolf, the "antica lupa" with her boundless hunger, kindred and interconnected symbols, though the one suggests the enticement that sets desire off on her wild course, the other the endless rapacity of the course itself (*Purgatorio,* XIX, 7–33; XX, 10–12).[22] Considered with regard to the temporal political order, cupidity is chiefly opposed to justice (*Monarchia,* I, xi, 11); but in respect to the eternal order and man's relation to the Creator, cupidity is the chief hindrance both to the natural desire for God impressed on the rational soul from the first moment of its existence, and to that more explicit desire for God—charity (*caritas*)—which is the response to God's own redemptive love revealed in Christ. In the latter respect, cupidity represents the

22. Cf. *Inferno,* I, 49–60; 94–111.

soul's loss of the Supreme Good through an endlessly
sterile, futile pursuit of lesser goods, the created things
that never slake its "natural thirst" (*Purgatorio,* XXI,
1–3).[23] In pursuit of these things which can never
fulfill it, the soul in effect is pursuing, not desire's fulfillment, but desire itself; it is desiring always to desire.[24] Such is the errant desire of fallen man; such
was the desire of Adam when he fell. In fact, such
desire *was* his fall, for in willing a freedom unchecked
by reason or the nature of things or the will of God,
Adam in effect willed simply to will; he desired simply
and endlessly to desire (*Paradiso,* VII, 25–27). This
barren desire is Adam's legacy to us all—a perpetual
outrunning of reason and ignoring of God, unless and
until God himself, on His own initiative, should come
to heal and raise up His fallen creatures. This God in
fact has done by the astounding method of Incarnation,
of becoming a man Himself:

> Until it pleased God's Word to come down to
> where He joined Himself, in person, to that
> nature, which had gone astray from its Maker,
> by sole act of His eternal love.

> (fin ch'al Verbo di Dio di scender piacque
> u' la natura, che dal suo fattore
>   s'era allungata, uní a sé in persona
>   co l'atto sol del suo etterno amore.)
>
>   (*Paradiso,* VII, 30–33)

With this last phrase we touch the properly Christian
theme of the divine love coming—or "running," as

23. Cf. *Convivio,* IV, xii, 14–17.
24. Cf. *Convivio,* III, xv, 9.

Dante puts it[25]—to meet human love, heal it, redirect and elevate it, and draw it to a perfect and eternal union with God. To pursue that theme would require another lecture. Let me conclude this one on the nature and workings of human love in Dante with a final stress on the idea that underlies all his mature philosophy and theology—that man of his nature loves and desires God, because the rational soul that makes him human is an immediate effect, and therefore an image, of God Himself, and thus of the eternal love whose *object* is God Himself. "Your life," says Beatrice to Dante,

> but your life the supreme Goodness directly breathes out, and makes it in love with Himself, so that henceforth it ever desires Him.

> (ma vostra vita sanza mezzo spira
>   la somma beninanza, e la innamora
>   di sé sí che poi sempre la disira.)
>   (*Paradiso*, VII, 142–44)

25. Cf. *Purgatorio*, XV, 67–69.

5.

Dramas of Selfhood in the Comedy

BY THOMAS M. GREENE

Professor of English and Comparative Literature,
Yale University

As we meet today to honor the anniversary of the
poet's birth, we can take satisfaction in the thought
that the academic form of our celebration would undoubtedly have pleased him. He was probably no
stranger to academic seances and rituals; there is some
evidence to authorize the picture one willingly forms
of him, attending lectures or disputations at Bologna
and Paris, and he himself may well have occupied a
lecturer's podium toward the end of his life to investi-
gate a certain delicate problem in geophysics. But our
ritual today is calculated to grace Dante's memory in
another way as well, as it would grace even the most
anti-academic poet, because our meeting demonstrates
our faith in the inexhaustibility of his work. To return,
after so many centuries of study, to the meditation of
his texts is really to bear witness that their meditation
is literally endless. That thought, in turn, must necessarily humble us should we seek for ultimate inter-

pretations; we must continue to remind ourselves that the pursuit of a classic earns no finality and that its end lies forever open.

The aspect of the *Comedy* which I want to explore this afternoon has to do with the peculiar ontology of those souls whom Dante encounters in the course of his pilgrimage. In each of these figures we can discern a kind of drama based on the paradox of his other-worldly being—namely, the paradox that he both is and is not his earthly self. This double truth invests the soul with a richly problematical relationship toward that former living self, and in every case the poet, with his unsurpassed dramatic sense, seizes upon the tensions which are thereby generated. As Dante conceived it, the afterlife confers upon each soul a new property, which has been of necessity lacking from his earthly existence and which is now set over against it. This new property might be called the *retrospective vision* upon his earthly self, a vision which he gains only from his experience after death and more precisely from the divine judgment upon his former living self. Without exception and without regard to the fate assigned him, his acquired perspective plays upon his memory, colors his judgment, and creates a new self-consciousness. Indeed, on Mount Purgatory, that retrospective vision, that fresh self-consciousness, acts as a means of redemption to alter the earthly self still further. That play of new vision upon the old identity constitutes the drama of the character's self-hood. One way of grasping that drama is to note his attitude toward his earthly name, and we shall have occasion to notice how deftly and variously Dante suggests those attitudes. Just as the soul both is and is not his living self, so the name fits and no longer fits.

These paradoxes are dramatized very early in the *Comedy,* in the opening exchange between Virgil and Dante. Virgil's first words in the poem—"No, not a man; I was once a man" (Non omo, omo già fui)— tend to dissociate his present self from his earthly past, and the remainder of his opening speech continues to stress that gap:

> I lived at Rome under the good Augustus, at the time of the false and deceiving gods. I was a poet.

> (vissi a Roma sotto 'l buono Augusto
> al tempo de li dei falsi e bugiardi.
> Poeta fui.)
>
> > *(Inferno,* I, 71–73)

Virgil no longer lives under false gods, but he is no longer a poet either. Dante's reply, however, insists on the continuity of Virgil's selfhood, shifting the temporal emphasis from past to present tense:

> Are you than that Virgil?
>
> (Or sei tu quel Virgilio?)
>
> > *(Inferno,* I, 79)

> You are my master and my author.
>
> (Tu se' lo mio maestro e 'l mio autore.)
>
> > *(Inferno,* I, 85)

Virgil in his own view has survived the greatness associated with his name, darkened as that greatness was by religious blindness; Virgil in Dante's eyes remains a living power. Both views are correct, and their disparity intensifies the sober pathos of Virgil's presence throughout the first two canticles.

Each of the canticles contains its own particular tension between retrospective vision and the continuing identity of the old earthly self. The tension peculiar to the sinners of the *Inferno* depends upon two principles. First, the sinner is incapable of true contrition for his transgressions—that is, contrition in the sense that the *Purgatorio* will illustrate. He is clearly capable of some vague regret in varying degrees, but he cannot by definition divorce himself from the sum of his sinfulness by a profound and total act of recommitment. No one in the *Inferno* uses a phrase like Arnaut Daniel's ("passada folor" [past folly]) to evoke his lifetime on earth. Each of the damned in some degree still wills and loves his sin. But cutting athwart that continuing passion is the second principle of his condition, namely, that he is incapable of doubting the propriety of his punishment. We may assume that Griffolino speaks for all the damned when he speaks of Minos "who may not err" (a cui fallar non lece). The sinner accepts the harshness of divine justice upon himself even as he clings to the habit which calls down that justice. Condemnation to hell confers upon him a form of self-knowledge, knowledge which may lead to self-loathing since it is helpless to alter his moral being. Not only the torment but also the pattern of evil within himself is fixed for eternity. He must exist between the clash of pride and ineffectual remorse, habit and disgust, memory of dignity and knowledge of debasement.

Thus when we encounter a formula like Capaneo's

—"As I was alive, so am I dead" (Qual io fui vivo, tal son morto), a phrase resonant with grandiose and fiercely self-centered obduracy—we are swept up in a swirl of ironies. First, there is the evident irony in such a boast from the lips of a former king, humbled forever in supine helplessness, passively exposed to a rain of fire. But there is also the crueler irony which Virgil formulates—that the obsessive rage of the blasphemer Capaneo is its own punishment, that the continuity of past and present which he vaingloriously asserts is a symptom of his damnation. Capaneo embodies that tragic rigidity of the personality common to all the damned, condemned as they are to repeat endlessly the gestures of their crippled loves. As they were alive, so *are* they dead, imprisoned within their compulsive memories, still bearing the evidence of whatever goodness or greatness they achieved—and ruined—on earth. But Capaneo, we may assume, understands as well as Griffolino that Minos may not err, that his torment *is* deserved, and we have to view his frenzied defiance as directed not only toward God but also toward that silent judgment within himself. In this sense he is *not* now as he was living; his fury is intensified by his retrospective vision, and his attempt to conceal his anguish only serves to reveal it. That is his final irony.

The tragedy of rigidity which Capaneo embodies so strikingly recurs in various forms throughout the *Inferno,* indeed, wherever it is possible to use the term "tragedy." We think at once of Farinata, all his august "virtù" entombed within a burning sepulcher, but how much more effectively entombed within his partisan passions! His famous immobility is a spiritual immobility, bound as he is to the incomplete loves of class and party and the city of Florence:

> that noble fatherland toward which I was perhaps too severe.

> (quella nobil patria . . .
> alla qual forse fui troppo molesto.)
> (*Inferno,* X, 26–27)

We have to picture him constrained for eternity within the limits of that "forse," straining against the hypothetical concession which is all his retrospective vision affords him. Nothing is more characteristic of him than his withholding his name in that first speech from which I just quoted. He refers to himself and to his past as though Dante the pilgrim should know him without any introduction, and yet he died the year before Dante was born. Virgil happily saves the situation by pronouncing this great man's name, for the only time in the canto or the poem: "See there Farinata who has risen" (Vedi là Farinata che s'è dritto) (*Inferno,* X, 32). Farinata is too proud to identify himself; more than that, he is too alone with his own identity, preoccupied still with a violent and fossilized past. His identity, the sum of that past, is in a sense all that exists for him, and it may well seem to him needless to tag reality with a simple name.

There is an alternative in the *Comedy* to the petrification of the damned personality, and it is "speranza" (hope). Speranza involves precisely that openness to conversion, that capacity for transforming the self, which the damned have failed to achieve on earth and

now cannot achieve. It appears in the *Inferno* only
negatively, but the *Purgatorio* reveals its crucial importance for the whole poem. Dante did not regard
it as the very greatest of the virtues, but it is the closest
to the action of his work. In the sphere of the Fixed
Stars, Beatrice says of Dante that the church militant
has no son more full of hope, and he in turn, when
he makes his valediction to Beatrice, begins by ad-
dressing her as the source of his hope. The argument
of the *Comedy* rests upon hope, upon the capacity of
every man for conversion and redemption, and the
pilgrimage of the poet symbolizes, as we know, this
universal alternative. He comes to represent the self
within each man which can escape this dark wood
about us, the self which can *turn* and change.

The Italian verb meaning "to turn" ("volgere") ac-
quires considerable moral significance in the *Comedy,*
where it is used to denote both a forsaking of the
straight way ("diritta via") and a return to it, until
finally, in the concluding sentence of the poem, the
straight way becomes circular and the main verb,
"volgeva," describes the will of the poet turned in the
perpetual wheel of celestial order. For the living individual on earth, burdened by sin, aided but not
determined by grace, the psychology of redemption
depends upon his ability to turn, to turn himself before
being turned in heaven. Hope depends upon a psychic
flexibility, a disposition to renew the self without denying the self. That flexibility is precisely what we miss
among the damned. They must abandon hope in hell
because they have abandoned it on earth, because they
have chosen to repeat themselves without a peripety.

The drama of Guido da Montefeltro hinges most poignantly upon the psychology of conversion, since Guido is one who apparently chose to turn but failed. Few personal histories in the *Inferno* are more affecting than his, as he tells it in the twenty-seventh canto—the turbulent life of action, the subsequent decision to join the Franciscan order, and then the debasing recall to politics through the false promises of absolution by Pope Boniface. Here the continuity of wickedness on earth seems anything but fixed and its persistence after death still more questionable. For Guido repeats his story in accents of regret which are restrained but unmistakable, and he concludes with a confession of remorse which is all the more haunting for its reticence:

> Thus I am lost here where you see me, and, so clothed, go in self-reproach.

> (per ch'io là dove vedi son perduto,
> e sì vestito, andando mi rancuro.)
> (*Inferno,* XXVII, 128–29)

In this ruin of a great spirit, tragically unredeemed, death has surely softened the rigidity of the sinner's disposition. Memory persists, to be sure; nobility also persists, along with a certain aristocratic courtesy, but very little evident depravity, and Guido's retrospective vision seems unusually lucid—so it appears, at least, on first reading. But the full implications of the text project a subtler, more ambiguous portrait and force us to reconsider certain details. Guido first accosts Dante out of curiosity about the politics of his native region, the Romagna, accosts him with an intensity not quite concealed by the elaborate courtliness of his language. Dante's reply in turn is so generous that

Guido finds himself obligated to answer the poet's questions about himself. At this point there arises an uneasy tension. We sense that this circumspect spirit has been drawn further into the exchange than he wished; we even discern that the fire which punishes him serves as a welcome concealment. Dante hints at this as he addresses him: "O soul who are hidden there below" (O anima che se' là giu nascosta) (*Inferno,* XXVII, 36). Clearly something of his earthly faith in connivance remains to Guido, and significantly it is only after a prudent calculation that he consents to identify himself. The calculation mistakenly assumes that Dante will never return to earth to damage his reputation. As on earth he lived by calculation, "the wisest and subtlest soldier of his time," wily and self-defeating, so in death his circumspection persists and goes astray. But in hell it appears as it is—an irrelevance, a compulsive mannerism of the personality, what the French call a *tic.* As we continue to scrutinize Guido, he reveals himself to be the brilliant, driven man he has always been, and his remorse shades into the regret of the trickster undone by baser trickery, a regret not for insufficient love but insufficient caution. His supposed conversion in life reveals itself as an impulse rather than a commitment; perhaps his hope itself rested on a calculation. He was duped not by the pope but by the habits of his moral disposition. Now his new self-knowledge mingles with an earthly fury at being outwitted, and Dante refrains from indicating which is stronger, the lucid judgment or the human spite.

Guido's reluctance to name himself is common among the damned; its ostensible cause is most often the sinner's concern for his reputation, but it also betrays an evasion of the deadly burden of selfhood. If Farinata withholds his name through obsessive pride, many more withhold theirs through shame and self-revulsion. Caccianemico the pander is representative; recognized, named, and questioned by Dante, he must shamefully confess his identity and his sin, with a rueful complaint at the jogging of his memory:

> I tell it unwillingly, but I am compelled by your well-informed speech, which makes me remember the old world.

> (Mal volentier lo dico;
> ma sforzami la tua chiara favella,
> che mi fa sovvenir del mondo antico.
> (*Inferno,* XVIII, 52–54)

He lumps together his name, the living world, and the fatal act which he proceeds to recall. Most secretive of all the spirits is the traitor Bocca degli Abàti, who conceals his name even under manhandling by the angry poet, only to be unmasked by a fellow sinner. But despite this furtive reluctance of the damned to acknowledge their names and histories, we encounter some who, on the contrary, hasten to reveal themselves. Vanni Fucci the thief, for example, identifies himself with a kind of hysterical bravado. He has chosen to bear the burden of his selfhood with a wild and astringent hilarity, as though to forestall and disarm disgust. The poet does not allow him to make a successful show of his bravado, however. The sham collapses when he recognizes Dante the pilgrim, and he mutters with bitter shame:

I regret more that you have caught me in the wretchedness in which you see me than when I was taken from the other life.

> (Più mi duol che tu m'hai colto
> ne la miseria dove tu mi vedi,
> che quando fui de l'altra vita tolto.)
> *(Inferno,* XXIV, 133–35)

He has pretended to accept himself, his violent past, his miserable present, but he cannot sustain the lie. The awareness of moral responsibility, the intolerable knowledge of being himself, is ironically and implacably revealed in its torment for all the demonic hysteria of his deception.

Brunetto Latini is among the few sinners who appear to accept themselves neither out of pride nor defiance, but from fortitude and resignation. Brunetto, unrecognized at first by Dante the pilgrim, seizes him by the hem of his coat and forces a confrontation. When the pilgrim makes out the beloved features of his former master, he cries out, "Are you here, Ser Brunetto?" (Siete voi qui, ser Brunetto?), mingling surprise, compassion, pleasure, dismay, and reluctance to believe, so that the spirit replies:

> O my son, may it not displease you if Brunetto Latini turns back with you a little and lets the troop pass by.

> (O figliuol mio, non ti dispiaccia
> se Brunetto Latini un poco teco
> ritorna in dietro e lascia andar la traccia.)
> *(Inferno,* XV, 31–33)

Brunetto seizes upon the name as Dante pronounces it and repeats it with a proud melancholy, insisting on it with a kind of bitter courage. He is resigned to the burden of wearing the distinguished name he has tarnished. Only in his valediction does there flicker a nuance of evasion, a hint that he too finds it intolerable to be as he now is:

> May my *Tesoro* be commended to you, in which I live still, and I ask nothing more.

> (Sieti raccomandato il mio Tesoro
> nel qual io vivo ancora, e più non cheggio.)
> *(Inferno,* XV, 119–20)

Brunetto imputes his life to his book in which, he says, he still lives, a phrase fusing his pride in that past achievement with the abnegation of present despair. Like all the damned he is frozen in the past, but he at least can cheer himself with the myth of another selfhood, a book which sums him up, a not altogether dead thing.

Up to this point we have been considering those sinners whose punishment it is to bear a name and, through the name, responsibility. But we ought to take note for a moment of those who are identified only vaguely or not at all. In a few cases Dante leads us to feel that he withholds the name because it has no actual referent, because the creature who bore the name achieved no moral individuality and thus no selfhood. This implication is of course clearest in the case of the so-called neutrals, who are punished outside of hell proper and who all remain unnamed. None of the spirits contained within the Inferno proper can be said to lack being as do the neutrals, and yet it is significant that one other circle contains no specified individuals. This is the fourth circle, where the hoarders and wasters are punished by forever rolling and clashing stones in two monotonous semicircles. Here the pilgrim expresses his desire to meet some who might be familiar to him, whereupon Virgil replies:

> You harbor a vain thought; the undiscerning life
> that made them filthy now makes them dark to
> any discernment.

> (Vano pensiero aduni:
> la sconoscente vita che i fé sozzi
> ad ogni conoscenza or li fa bruni.)
> *(Inferno,* VII, 52–54)

The key word is "undiscerning" (sconoscente), which implies an inability to distinguish good from evil; the undiscerning existence of these souls on earth now renders their recognition impossible. Dante must have distinguished the undiscerning life from the perfectly neutral life; he must have considered these hoarders and wasters to have been, in Eliot's phrase, men enough to damn themselves. Yet in their utter anonymity they share something of the contempt directed to the neutrals; whatever identities they once possessed are withered and gray. They exist only in terms of their vice, which they eternally assert in mutual recrimination: "Why do you hoard?" "Why do you throw away?" Beyond these simple habits, Dante says, they are unknowable.

The view of Dante's characterization which I should like to emerge from these remarks is a little at variance with another view which has justly enjoyed considerable prestige in our time, and before proceeding further, I ought to make clear to what extent I really mean to take issue with it. According to this view, the image of the soul after death sums up simply and completely the complex truth of its life on earth, defining and fulfilling the essence of that life. The theory was first formulated, to the best of my knowledge, by Hegel, who in his *Lectures on Aesthetics* speaks of the *Comedy* as follows:

> What is otherwise most perishable and evanescent in the living world receives here a completely epic form objectively based on its own innermost life, and adjudged in its worth and unworth by the supreme notion of all, that is God. For as individuals were in their life and suffering, their opinions and accomplishment on Earth, so are they here set before us for ever consolidated, as it were, into images of bronze.[1]

Hegel's conception is worked out very powerfully and suggestively on the page from which this quotation is drawn, in a discussion which continues to stress the static character of Dante's universe, "a world that is for ever determined." The theory of the soul as a

1. G. W. F. Hegel, *The Philosophy of Fine Art*, trans. F. P. B. Osmaston (4 vols. London, 1920), 4, 184.

"bronze image" of its living self requires that stasis. Although he alludes to the protagonist "wandering" through this changeless world, Hegel's emphasis throughout on an eternal fixity recalls Dante's own formulation of his subject as "the state of souls after death." But if Dante authorizes this kind of static interpretation, he also suggests in the same document (the famous letter to Can Grande) a more dynamic subject of his work. This suggestion—veiled to be sure, but almost transparently—appears in the discussion of allegory, where Dante uses a passage from Scripture to illustrate the four levels of interpretation. The passage he selects begins, "When Israel went out of Egypt" (*In exitu Israel de Aegypto*), a passage which he interprets to refer on its several levels to redemption. Now it has generally been assumed that Dante did not choose this scriptural passage as his example arbitrarily, but rather meant to suggest that redemption was also the theme of his own work.[2] If we accept this assumption, as I think we should, we are left with two subjects—one, the dynamic, involving a process, redemption, and the other, the static subject, the state of souls after death. To point out this double focus of the *Comedy* as its author conceived it is not of course to imply any confusion in his mind or his art; the two subjects or aspects are brilliantly and harmoniously fused. But this double focus may well lead us to consider incomplete an interpretation which neglects or

2. For a recent study of Dante's use of the passage within the *Comedy,* see Charles Singleton, "In Exitu Israel de Aegypto," in *Dante,* ed. John Freccero, Twentieth Century Views (Englewood Cliffs, 1965).

denies either aspect, the stasis or the process. Hegel, in fact, denies the process; he really denies the importance of hope. He writes:

> We have not here one progressive action, individual and exclusive, on the broad basis of the entire poem: what, however, we do get in a conspicuous degree in this Epos is the most secure articulation and consummate finish. Instead of a particular event, it has for its subject matter the eternal event, the absolute end, the Divine Love in its imperishable eventuality, and in its unalterable circles of relation to the object.[3]

By rejecting the action of the poem, Hegel rejects the aspect figured by the line "In exitu Israel de Aegypto"; he rejects the meaning of Dante's pilgrimage, which is not a "wandering" but a deliberate progression toward Love, and in rejecting this, he exposes the insufficiency of his conception.

This conception has been revived in our time, expanded, and supported with wide learning by Erich Auerbach. Auerbach belongs to that distinguished company of students who have renewed the living presence of Dante for our century. His revival of the Hegelian conception is a magisterial exercise of exegesis and erudition, such that no summary or quotation can adequately represent it. Following Hegel, he regards the soul after death as fixed in an eternal situation which perfects and reveals the truth of that soul's life:

3. Hegel, p. 184.

We behold an intensified image of the essence of their being, fixed for all eternity in gigantic dimensions, behold it in a purity and distinctness which could never for one moment have been possible during their lives upon earth.[4]

In support of this view, Auerbach is able to point to the figural interpretation of history which he finds to pervade medieval exegesis of Scripture, and he goes on to characterize the *Comedy* as a figural poem. This means among other things that for Dante the life of each individual, however actual and concrete during its unfolding on earth, reaches its full definition and fulfillment *only* in the beyond, where its final truth sums up and fixes eternally the life that has prefigured it.

The world beyond . . . is God's design in active fulfillment. In relation to it, earthly phenomena are on the whole merely figural, potential, and requiring fulfillment. This also applies to the individual souls of the dead: it is only here, in the beyond, that they attain fulfillment and the true reality of their being. Their career on earth was only the figure of this fulfillment.[5]

The theory is nobly conceived and argued with eloquence and passion, but although the thought is more sophisticated and the learning more assured, Auerbach's formulation, strictly interpreted, seems to me

4. Erich Auerbach, *Mimesis: The Representation of Reality in Western Literature,* trans. W. Trask (Princeton, 1953), p. 192.
5. Ibid., p. 196.

basically vulnerable to the same criticism as Hegel's. Auerbach does not, of course, miss the meaning of the poet's pilgrimage; he does not miss the unity of the central action. Nonetheless, like Hegel, he does not sufficiently allow for process, specifically for the process of purgation as it is dramatized in the second canticle. It is simply not true to assert that the souls on Mount Purgatory are fixed for eternity; on the contrary, they are creatures in transition, acutely conscious of the transition. We do not, to be sure, actually see any soul transformed before our eyes; only Dante the pilgrim changes as we read, and for our purposes he is irrelevant, being alive. But even if the souls are static as we meet them, they are in upward movement from the perspective of God, and Dante could not have permitted himself to regard them as finally perfected or fulfilled. Artistically fulfilled they may be, but metaphysically they are not, and the figural theory supposes that the two fulfillments coincide.

A second objection to a narrow interpretation of Auerbach is already implicit in my remarks on the *Inferno*. We surely do not see the essence of a character's life fixed after death with "purity and distinctness"; we see it filtered through the retrospective vision, the acquired judgment directed backward, a judgment which is not prefigured by anything in life. In the *Inferno,* moreover, the judgment is itself incomplete, as we see it at work within each character's consciousness, given room within that consciousness to the degree that the character can tolerate it. Much of the force and subtlety in Dante's portraits lie precisely in that dialectic of the divided mind. To see the mind monistically is to suppress the drama of its dialectic.

One more example from the *Inferno* may serve to clarify the issue and possibly suggest a resolution. Consider the elaborate formula which Pier della Vigna employs to denote his own suicide:

> My mind, through its taste for scorn, thinking to escape from scorn by dying, made me, just, unjust to myself.

> (L'animo mio, per disdegnoso gusto,
>   credendo col morir fuggir disdegno,
>   ingiusto fece me contra me giusto.)
>   (*Inferno,* XIII, 70–72)

The labored intricacies, the deliberate periphrasis, and the complex introversion do indeed render the man that Pier must have been. All the tics, all the obsessions of the man are preserved in his speech; for him as for the other sinners, his history is a cell which preserves and confines him as he was. Figural interpretation could well point to this sentence and to the canto as a whole as structures capturing brilliantly the sum of a person and a life. But to stop at this point would be to miss the subtlest ironies of the spiraling auto-criticism. "L'animo mio . . . ingiusto fece me contra me giusto." Pier is one of the souls in hell whose retrospective vision is most lucid and most severe, and yet he is chiefly concerned with justifying himself, with an irrelevance—the exoneration of his name in history. The phrase "disdegnoso gusto" represents a pride that he has not lost, although he thinks he has, and he continues to waver between self-laceration and self-indulgence.

This wavering is a function of Pier's existence after death, but it is by no means untypical of the man as he lived on earth. In this consideration perhaps one can discern common ground between the two interpretations in question. The recurrent act of retrospective judgment after death is not prefigured on earth; it is a new component of the consciousness. But the character of that judgment might well be said to be prefigured, that is, the harshness, clarity, and intensity of the judgment as it plays upon the old persisting self. These qualities of the retrospective judgment clearly depend upon the soul's peculiar earthly personality, at least in the *Inferno*. In other words, one could not predict on earth the existence of that judgment, but once informed, one might predict a given individual's use of it. If we choose to understand the figural theory in this somewhat broader sense, then it remains an illuminating and profound insight, particularly into the *Inferno*.

The dialectic within the self shifts considerably in the *Purgatorio,* and here the reader has to make a corresponding shift in his expectations. The judgment upon the living self becomes an instrument of self-transformation, and the personality slowly yields to its refinement. Having proved itself supple on earth by the act of conversion, the soul gradually surrenders or redirects its compulsive passions. The name it has borne on earth must be stretched in order to follow the soul's progressive evolution. Not without flutterings of nostalgia, the individual grows less recognizable. The continuity of style and gesture fades away, and memory itself is cleansed at the summit of the mountain.

The souls here tend to regard their very names as relics, outworn appendages, symbols of brief renown gained by achievements no longer worth the praise. "Your fame is the color of grass that comes and goes" (La vostra nominanza è color d'erba,/che viena e va) (*Purgatorio,* XI, 115–16) says Oderisi d'Agobbio on the terrace of pride. One figure after another identifies himself in the past tense, almost as though his name were an embarrassing necessity for intercourse with a living man:

> I was a Lombard, and was called Marco.
> (Lombardo fui, e fu' chiamato Marco.)
> > (*Purgatorio,* XVI, 46)

> I was called Currado Malaspina.
> (Fui chiamato Currado Malaspina.)
> > (*Purgatorio,* VIII, 118)

> I was not sapient although I was called Sapia.
> (Savia non fui, avvegna che Sapía
>   fossi chiamata.)
> > (*Purgatorio,* XIII, 109–10)

> Down there I was called Hugh Capet.
> (Chiamato fui di là Ugo Ciappetta.)
> > (*Purgatorio,* XX, 49)

The repetition of the participle "chiamato" in each case seems to imply that naming was an arbitrary habit of the world which failed to reach the essence of the individual. Yet many other characters fail to make this implication and instead introduce themselves in the present tense. Once again we have the double truth: the soul is and is not its earthly self. Again we must try to grasp that paradox as it affects this realm and this canticle.

In trying to understand, it is helpful to remember the doctrine of Saint Bernard: that man as originally created was endowed with both goodness and greatness—*rectitudo* and *magnitudo*—that his greatness consisted in his capacity for salvation, and that after the fall man lost his goodness but not his greatness. The souls undergoing purgation must be regarded in Bernard's terms as retaining their greatness and recapturing their goodness. They must recognize this in some way themselves; in spite of the tears they shed for their past errors, they must respect the greatness in themselves which God has created and has given them the grace to preserve. They must be aware of their own essential worth, not only as members of a species but also as individuals who lived given lives at given times and places. Contrition may not blot out self-respect, and memory need not bring only pain.

Having recognized this, however, the soul who is purged must realize that in lacking the original goodness, he lacked one of the basic properties of manhood. To realize himself fully as a man, he must achieve a moral perfection which will dwarf the self he has been on earth. While still caring about the world and the man he was in that world, the soul must withdraw far enough to see it within an immense context. Yet all the while he is bound to it quite directly by his need of earthly prayers to speed his purgation.

Thus the dialectic within these souls lies between their enlightened hope and those earthly affections yet unrefined, affections which would face them backward and downward. But here the dialectic is not vicious and sterile as in hell, but creative and serene. We as earthly readers prize the narrow attachment, the local affection yet unrefined, even as we accept the beautiful propriety of its transcendence.

Seeing how much remains unrefined in certain characters, we are struck by the wonder of redemption, which seems to require such a small gesture from the living man. That wonder is embodied in the smile of Manfred, the handsome and courtly king who died excommunicate. He appears to the poet on the lowest slope of the mountain and asks, as though preparing a surprise, if Dante has ever seen him.

> When I had humbly disclaimed ever having seen him, he said, "Now look" and showed me a wound above his breast. Then he said smiling: "I am Manfred."

> (Quand' i' mi fui umilmente disdetto
>   d'averlo visto mai, el disse: "Or vedi";
>   e mostrommi una piaga a sommo 'l petto.
> Poi sorridendo disse: "Io son Manfredi."
>   (*Purgatorio,* III, 109–12)

The wound above the breast is Manfred's death wound, which he received in a battle fatal not only to himself but to his cause and his family. He points to the wound as a kind of identification, as though Dante, having seen it, would find it less difficult to believe that this was indeed Manfred before his eyes. However, the wound also serves to recall the violence and worldliness of Manfred's earthly career and thus renders his salvation more incredible, that is to say, more wonderful. He is among the first of those who are encountered on the mountain, and something of this wonder and this smile hovers faintly over the whole realm. He really smiles at the wonder of metamorphosis, and the sins he terms "horrible" remain with him to heighten the miracle and deepen the smile. His conversion occurred at the very end of his dissolute life, as he lay on the field of battle, defeated and dying. He appears now a miraculous symbol, gracious, courteous, and, we must believe, truly repentant. Yet he is the same man: "I *am* Manfred."

It is reassuring that the very last-named of the souls in the *Purgatorio* betrays his past history in no less forceful and unmistakable a manner—through his language. This is the Provençal poet Arnaut Daniel, whose speech of eight lines is spoken in his own tongue. His appearance on the terrace of the lustful is prepared by Dante's master Guido Guinizelli, who points out Arnaut, without naming him, as the finest of the vernacular makers. As Guido disappears again into the depths of the refining fire, the two poets are left facing one another as courteous strangers. Dante speaks first. He has understood from Guido that this unidentified figure, like themselves, belonged once to the elite of the "cuori gentili," the learned in love, and so his address is phrased with a preciosity reminiscent of that elite:

I advanced a little toward him who had been pointed out and said that my desire was preparing a gracious place for his name.

(Io mi feci al mostrato innanzi un poco,
e dissi ch'al suo nome il mio disire
apparecchiava grazioso loco.)
(*Purgatorio*, XXVI, 136–38)

Arnaut's reply in turn seems to catch the implications of Dante's elegant language but to reject subtly its preciosity. He sees the pilgrim as a follower of Guinizelli and a member of that elite he now condemns. "I regard that past folly with grief," he says. "I beg you . . . remember my pain while you still have time." There is almost a delicate reproof of that ritual language whose elaborations he has outgrown. Yet even as he says this, his own speech betrays its elegant habits. Purged of its esoterism and deepened by suffering, his language answers Dante's with a corresponding courtliness:

Your courteous request affords me such pleasure that I neither can nor wish to conceal myself from you. I am Arnaut who weep and go singing.

(Tan m'abellis vostre cortes deman,
qu'ieu no me puesc ni voill a vos cobrire.
Ieu sui Arnaut, que plor e vau cantan.)
(*Purgatorio*, XXVI, 142–44)

Arnaut's tears are for the "passada folor," the cult of an incomplete love, and yet as he sings in hope, his accents derive from that cult. Despite the pain of his retrospective vision, he is still Arnaut, still a Provençal, still a poet, still in some sense a "cor gentile," as he too withdraws into the refining fire.

Shortly thereafter, Virgil also vanishes. The drama of *his* selfhood in the *Comedy* is itself a subject for an essay, and today I can only suggest one of its minor aspects, having to do again with the use of his name. It is a curious fact that after the first canto of the *Inferno,* Virgil's name tends to drop out of the canticle. He is commonly addressed by his companion as "Maestro," and in the third person he is called "lo duca," "lo mio maestro," or some comparable epithet. After Dante's first cry of recognition the name "Virgilio" disappears for eighteen cantos, and throughout the *Inferno* it appears again only four times. It seems that the poet deliberately avoided naming this crucial figure who speaks and acts in all of the thirty-four cantos, and we can only speculate about his reasons. It may be that he was consciously concerned with creating a new fictive character who, to be successful, could not be identified too insistently at the outset with an actual historical person. We never for one moment forget, of course, that the poet's guide is indeed Virgil, the poet and sage of antiquity, but we are led progressively to understand him in his new role as instructor and guide through a world the ancient Virgil never knew.

In the *Purgatorio,* a new epithet is used frequently— "il poeta"—a title whose resonance would perhaps have been dissipated in the *Inferno.* But here the name Virgilio also appears with much greater frequency, perhaps with the implication that only in this realm will such a name be recognized and revered, as indeed first Sordello and later Statius revere it. The three recognition scenes—Dante's, Sordello's, Statius'—echoing and mirroring each other, punctuate the Virgil drama and measure his evolution as a character. The Statius episode in particular reintroduces the historical aspect of Virgil, the antique poet and seer, only to impress us with how much more he has become in Dante's poem, how much more living, humane, gracious, and melancholy a presence. When at last Dante the pilgrim discovers his master's disappearance, the name Virgilio is repeated over and over again, five times in ten lines, three times in three lines:

> But Virgil had left us bereft of himself, Virgil my sweetest father, Virgil to whom I gave myself for my salvation.

> (Ma Virgilio n'avea lasciati scemi
>   di sé, Virgilio dolcissimo patre,
>   Virgilio a cui per mia salute die'mi.)
>   (*Purgatorio,* XXX, 49–51)

A moment earlier, Dante had quoted the *Aeneid* in a kind of instinctive tribute to its author, but now, faced with his loss, it is not the author who is missed but the "dolcissimo patre," the man as he lived in *this* poem. The name Virgilio, so rich in specific associations when it is first pronounced, has been reinvested with new meaning and new life. According to the poem's doctrine, Virgil must exist without hope and without change, but in fact Dante grants him through his *art* that metamorphosis which theology could not allow.

His name is last pronounced in the *Purgatorio* by Beatrice, at the critical transition of the poem, even as she orients Dante's thoughts away from his lost guide. In the same breath she names Dante himself for the only time in the poem, and then, after a pause, herself:

> Dante, because Virgil departs weep not yet, weep not yet.
>
> (Dante, perchè Virgilio se ne vada,
>   non pianger anco, non pianger ancora.)
>   (*Purgatorio,* XXX, 55–56)

> Look well; I am, I am indeed Beatrice.
> (Guardaci ben! Ben son, ben son Beatrice.)
>   (*Purgatorio,* XXX, 73)

The dramatic introduction of the poet's own name seems to insist on his identity with the child who first loved her and the man who celebrated her, but her own name, pronounced with so much emphasis ("Ben son, ben son Beatrice") seems to answer an unspoken doubt in his mind whether this apparition is indeed the soul of his beloved. She is partly concealed by her veil, but even without it there would be grounds for doubt and wonder in the strangeness and splendor of her epiphany and in the new stern authority of her manner. She has grown in beauty, virtue, and radiance; she is transfigured by beatitude. Nevertheless in the eyes of her lover and in the eyes of God, she remains the same creature; she is indeed Beatrice.

In the *Inferno,* selfhood is fixed; in the *Purgatorio,* refined. For the *Paradiso,* one must have recourse to a word Dante coined; there, the self is "trasumanato." It is "transhumanized"; it passes beyond humanity. In heaven, the individual finds the place of rest which defines him for eternity; his intellect and will, already purified, attain the supreme object of knowledge and desire, and in the double act of knowing and loving, the individual passes beyond his mortal self. To pass beyond, however, is from another perspective to actualize the self, to achieve finally and truly one's full identity. From the retrospective vision of heaven, the earthly man appears as an immature stage in the soul's spiritual development. He is, we might say, on the far side of metamorphosis. Thus when Dante encounters the first soul in heaven, Piccarda Donati, he explains his failure to recognize her in terms of her transformation by a "non so che divino," and Piccarda herself, out of tact rather than vanity, alludes to her own growth in beauty. We are constantly aware of the heavenly souls as creatures emergent from a process—the transhumanizing of love.

Such a process might seem to threaten the color, the particularity of the person, and it is doubtless true that fewer great individuals appear *as* individuals in the third canticle than in either of the preceding. The personal history of the soul loses a little of its distinctness in the engulfing vision of the eye and the mind. The souls who appear to the poet are not simply fulfillments of their former selves, as the figural theory would have it; they are extensions, emptied of the tics and compulsions of this life, emptied even of repentance. Yet despite this emptiness, it is in this canticle that the poet pays his highest tribute to the diversity and uniqueness of the human creature. "Various voices make sweet accords" (Diverse voci fanno dolci note) (*Paradiso,* VI, 124) says Justinian, and the same thought is echoed by Charles Martel. Citizenship is impossible, he says—and by citizenship he means a just society—"unless men live below in various ways for various tasks" (se giù non si vive/diversamente per diversi offici) (*Paradiso,* VIII, 118–19). But Dante sets the final stamp upon the value of the single individual in the Empyrean, where each soul is made visible in its human form, the symbol of its separate identity. There, where so much is vindicated, the uniqueness of the person also prevails. In other words, Dante seems to make a distinction, not very congenial to our modern minds, between identity and personality; personality tends to pale in heaven, but identity is sustained.

The striking, even surprising aspect of the blessed souls is the pleasure they take in identifying themselves, a pleasure beyond the suspicion of egoism. Despite the process of transformation through which they have passed, they are quite certain of who they are, and if they are bound to the poet by any particular tie, the joy of their self-revelation can scarcely be contained. If in hell one's identity is the heaviest of burdens, in heaven it is a source of joy. This joyful sense of the self must explain, I think, the curious opening of the Cacciaguida episode. The crusader-martyr, ancestor of the poet, insists on a kind of ritual here. He recognizes his descendant, who does not, quite naturally, recognize him, but whose eagerness to learn his name increases with the soul's expressions of gladness. Cacciaguida says, in effect, in language of elaborate formality: "You think that I know your wish without your formulating it. I do indeed know it, but in order to heighten my joy still further, let your voice express the wish aloud." Whereupon the poet, in equally formal language, does indeed ask the soul his name. Only then does Cacciaguida reveal his kinship, and only after further delay is the name finally pronounced. The ritual of self-revelation with its ceremonious language, its calculated and drawn-out solemnity, intensifies the exalted excitement of the meeting. Neither Cacciaguida nor any other soul in heaven has so lost himself in the contemplation of God as to forget his private bonds of friendship and blood. So the young king Charles Martel equally responds with joy, not so much when he recognizes and approaches the poet, but a moment later when the poet asks, "Tell me, who are you?" (Deh, chi siete?)

The answer to that question is given by means of an elaborate formula which effectively satisfies the asker but which does not in fact contain the speaker's name, Carlo Martello. Indeed, the name appears nowhere in the text of the poem. In the *Paradiso,* as nowhere else, Dante is extraordinarily reticent with names. Thus along with Charles Martel, St. John the Evangelist remains unnamed during his encounter with Dante, as do St. Benedict and Adam. Others, like St. Peter, are only named long after their first appearances. The soul's earthly designation seems to be considered increasingly a mere linguistic accident. This distrust is extended to the very name of the Deity, Who, according to Adam, was once called "I" and later "El":

> and this is fitting, because the usage of mortal men is like a leaf on a branch, which falls and another comes.

> (e ciò convene,
> ché l'uso de' mortali è come fronda
> in ramo, che sen va e altra vene.)
> *(Paradiso,* XXVI, 136–38)

Language, like all products of human reason, is mutable.

The name in the *Paradiso* tends to give place to a rhetorical figure which is intended apparently to transcend the mutable and the arbitrary. This figure is periphrasis, which indicates a character's identity through some elaborately wrought circumlocution. Thus St. Thomas Aquinas introduces the soul of Solomon, not by name but as

> the exalted mind to which such deep wisdom was granted that if the truth be true, a second never arose to see as much.

> (l'alta mente u' sì profondo
> saver fu messo, che se 'l vero è vero
> a veder tanto non surse il secondo.)
> *(Paradiso,* X, 112–14)

Such a description is not haphazard; it is essential to the style of the *Paradiso.* Indeed, it is not too much to say that the style of this canticle is basically periphrastic, that it describes and identifies not by the common substantive or proper noun but rather by the crucial property of the thing or the person.[6] The periphrasis is a kind of riddle which only the enlightened reader can solve, but it is also, as Dante employs it in this canticle, a gesture of praise. It is the trope of both "intelletto" and "amore," mind and love, which instructs but also caresses as it names. Without quite dispensing with names, Dante's language in the *Paradiso* presses beyond them to the essence of selfhood, the critical achievement or that peculiar aspect which reveals the inner, genuine individual. Such a technique unobtrusively asserts the unity of the soul's existence, juxtaposing and joining as it does past and present, created and transhumanized, Solomon alive and Solomon in heaven.

Thus by rhetoric as well as doctrine and action, Dante defines the condition of the soul "trasumanato." The *Paradiso* makes fully clear the nature of man's choice on earth. On the one hand, he may exist with himself for eternity in his centripetal, monotonous identity, imprisoned by memory, divided against himself, tormented by a punishment which itself symbolizes a force within him. On the other hand, he may choose to exist centrifugally, freed from the ravages of memory, from the oppression, though not the greatness, of

6. My emphasis here is slightly different from that of Mr. Scaglione, who quite properly stresses the metaphoric texture of the style of the *Paradiso*. It would perhaps require further discussion to make the proper distinctions and clarifications, but I suspect that our apparent disagreement is only superficial. In very many cases, the periphrasis is metaphoric. The only real question to be decided is which trope subsumes the other.

selfhood. The modern reader who does not share Dante's world-view may find something heroically human in the stubborn obsessions of the damned and something distastefully pallid in the joy of the blessed. Yet Dante wrote as though he understood that modern weariness with the self which was discovered by the Romantics and which brought even Hopkins to write: "Self-yeast of spirit a dull dough sours." Dante's alternative to self-yeast of spirit was the daily bread, the "cotidiana manna," of grace. For the modern man who seeks a third alternative, the myth of the *Comedy* remains profoundly relevant, since his experience also will constitute a drama of self-consciousness, a dynamic of rigidity and change, and it lasts only as long as it stays open, as long as hope bears a touch of green (mentre che la speranza ha fior del verde) (*Purgatorio*, III, 135).

6.

Imagery and Thematic Patterns in Paradiso *XXIII*

BY ALDO SCAGLIONE
Visiting Professor of Italian,
Yale University

The history of Dante's reception could illustrate in an exemplary manner the historical conditioning of literary criticism.[1] In asserting the poetic merits of the real, the sinful, the violent in the *Inferno,* De Sanctis was winning for his time the long battle for the emancipation of the negative, the irrational, and the primitive that had become part of the Romantic cause. That position was soon felt to demand a searching revision, and we have ultimately witnessed the response to a new historical need in the assertion of the ideal, even intellectual, nature of art. This has been typically achieved through a revaluation of the *Paradiso.*[2] De

1. An authoritative voice was recently heard to the effect that "historicism" has long been ready for liquidation, but, perhaps seen from a different angle, it seems stronger than ever. See René Wellek quoting Auerbach and Troeltsch in *Concepts of Criticism* (New Haven and London, 1963), pp. 13 and 20.

2. See, for the history of Dante criticism, B. Croce, *La poesia di Dante* (8th ed. Bari, 1956), Appendix; F. Maggini

Sanctis had, with his characteristic firmness, stressed
the aesthetic qualities of the text, and in this sense at
least, one can regard Croce's intervention as the cul-
mination of his method. This has given way to an
insistent return to the intellectual fabric of the divine
poem and, consequently, to a mode of reading that
would appear much closer, mutatis mutandis, to the
way the Trecento must have reacted to the poem. The
change in approach has undeniable merits, and our
understanding of this uniquely complex poem has
thereby gained immeasurably both in depth and in
refinement, but there are obvious dangers inherent in
overtasking this method.

One recalls that the first qualifier in the famous
epitaph attributed to Giovanni del Virgilio was "theologian": (Theologus Dantes, nullius dogmatis expers/
quod foveat claro philosophia sinu," and then, only
then, "gloria musarum).[3] More explicitly, and so much
more vividly, Benvenuto da Imola tells us that on
Dante's passing through the streets of Paris people
would point at him and identify him in different ways:

---

in *Questioni e Correnti di Storia Letteraria,* ed. Momigliano
(Milan, 1949), pp. 123–66; S. A. Chimenz in *Letteratura
Italiana. I Maggiori, 1* (Milan, 1956), 70–84; A. Vallone,
La Critica dantesca contemporanea (Pisa, 1953).

3. "Dante the theologian, master of every part of the
philosophic creed . . . glory of the Muses." Aldo Rossi has
been engaged in a brilliant attempt to prove that this epitaph,
as well as the whole bucolic correspondence between Dante
and del Virgilio, are an all too successful forgery by Boccaccio. He promises a book-length "indictment" soon; in the
meantime, see his articles in *Paragone, 13* (1962), 3–41;
Studi Danteschi, 40 (1963), 133–278; *Scritti su G. Boccaccio*
(Florence, 1964), pp. 20–62.

" 'Come, come,' some would say, 'Behold the philosopher!' But others would say: 'Behold the theologian!' And others still: 'Behold the poet!' " (Aliqui enim dicebant: "Veni, vide philosophum"; aliqui: "Vide theologum"; aliqui dicebant: "Vide poetam.")[4] Thus the majority seemed inclined to see first the thinker in Dante. It is a fate that has befallen other great poets and artists, among them even Homer and Dostoevsky.

What concerns us here is that the *theologus Dantes* has now come back quite strongly, and yet more than one demurrer has been heard from authoritative quarters.[5] Indeed, many feel that we might do well to turn back to the *vide poetam,* not in order to neglect the intellectual content of the work, the relevance of which must be firmly held even to the understanding of the

4. Cf. M. Barbi, *Problemi di critica dantesca, Seconda Serie* (*1920–1937*) (Florence, 1941), p. 453.

5. See one from a philosopher well versed in medieval thought and cultural history, R. McKeon's "Poetry and Philosophy in the Twelfth Century," in *Critics and Criticism,* ed. R. S. Crane (Chicago, 1952), p. 298: the twelfth century witnessed poet-philosophers just as the fifteenth did, whereas in the thirteenth century the two activities again became separate; thus Thomas Aquinas and Bonaventure remained philosophers even while they wrote excellent poetry, while "Dante, the great philosophic poet of the period, is not a philosopher by the crucial test that, despite the philosophic doctrines that crowd his poem, scholars have been unable to agree concerning what his attitude toward the philosophers he uses is."

Erich Auerbach's sound way of putting the problem contains a subtle distinction which only apparently contradicts the above: "The *Comedy* is an eminently philosophical work, not so much because of the actual philosophical doctrines set forth in it as because the spirit of those doctrines compels Dante to write philosophically." See his *Dante: Poet of the Secular World* (German ed., 1929), trans. R. Manheim (Chicago, 1961), p. 157.

poetry, but in order to see the elements of the poem in their proper perspective.

In prominent position among the prerequisites for the appreciation of a poem qua poem, one ought to place the understanding of its imagery. Even if we consider the mass of purely impressionistic literature of which Dante has been a favorite target, as well as the less relevant multitude of mere paraphrases of the text, it is surprising how comparatively little attention has been devoted to the imagery in Dante. Italian scholars have contributed less than others on this subject. Only five or six book-length studies have covered this important aspect of the poem in the last hundred years, and even the most extensive of these, which happens to be the latest in the series, leaves many things unsaid and more than one side of the question unexplored.[6] In America a scattered group of brief but

6. Cf. G. Franciosi, "Dell'evidenza dantesca studiata nelle metafore, nelle similitudini e ne' simboli," Atti dell'-Accademia di Modena (Modena, 1872), reprinted in Franciosi, *Scritti danteschi* (Florence, 1876), pp. 167–299, and Franciosi, *Nuova raccolta di scritti danteschi* (Parma, 1889); L. Venturi, *Le similitudini dantesche ordinate, illustrate e confrontate* (Florence, 1874, 2d ed. 1889, 3d ed. 1911); G. Acquaticci, *Le Gemme della Divina Commedia dichiarate e illustrate* (Cingoli, 1895); A. Sacchetto, "Le similitudini della *Divina Commedia*" and "Similitudini e dissimilitudini dantesche," *Il Giornale Dantesco, 27* and *28* (1924 and 1925), 346–51, 274–81; reprinted with an additional paper in Sacchetto, *Note e letture dantesche* (Padua, 1934), pp. 1–50, and in Sacchetto, *Il gioco delle immagini in Dante* (Florence, 1947); F. Olivero, "The Poetical Image in Dante," *Il Giornale Dantesco, 27* (1924), 248–62; "A Study on the Metaphor in Dante," ibid., *28* (1925), 61–84, 176–79; *The Representation of the Image in Dante* (Turin, 1936); *La rappresentazione dell' immagine in Dante,* trans. A. Benedetti (Turin, 1936, 1940); F. Maggini, "Associazioni etimologiche

pertinent interventions have been occasioned by some rather hasty and not too accurate remarks by T. S. Eliot, which have been inflated somewhat out of proportion and severely criticized.[7]

Let us center our attention on a particular case of imagery, the simile, which in Dante can become, at times, exceedingly elaborate in both content and form —and by form I refer specifically to syntactic structure as well as stylistic and rhetorical devices. An example of syntactic complexity or rather ambiguity is found in *Purgatorio,* VIII, 1–6 ("Era già l'ora che volge il disio . . ."), if one accepts Pagliaro's attempted reinterpretation.[8] We have an example of extended

---

nelle immagini di Dante," *Lingua Nostra,* 6 (1944–45), 25–28; Yvonne Batard, *Dante, Minerve et Apollon, Les images de la Divine Comédie* (Paris, 1952); Irma Brandeis, "Metaphor in the *Divine Comedy,*" *Hudson Review,* 8 (1956), 557–75; for a very personal approach, see D. Sayers, "The Poetry of the Image in Dante and Charles Williams," *Further Papers on Dante* (New York, 1957), pp. 183–204. Miss Brandeis has reprinted her paper in Brandeis, *The Ladder of Vision* (Garden City, 1960 and 1962), pp. 143–64; the remainder of this volume is also valuable for its insights into general as well as particular questions pertaining to imagery.

7. T. S. Eliot, *Dante* (London, 1929), esp. pp. 24–25; also as "Dante" in *Selected Essays* (New York, 1934), pp. 205–06. Cf. T. A. FitzGerald, "Dante's Figures of Speech," *Italica, 28* (1941), 120–23; Brandeis, n. 6 above; James Applewhite, "Dante's Use of the Extended Simile in the *Inferno,*" *Italica, 41* (1964), 294–309, esp. p. 295.

8. A. Pagliaro, "Ritmo e sintassi nel linguaggio dantesco," *Altri Saggi di Critica Semantica* (Messina–Florence, 1961), pp. 287–95. In my opinion, however, the syntactical conjectures proposed by Pagliaro are seriously weakened by a comparison between *Purgatorio,* VIII, 1–6, and *Paradiso,* XXIII, 1–6, which seem to offer a similar syntactic habit in *lo dí* and *la notte* as temporal complements and the delayed relative *che.*

simile in *Inferno,* XXIV, 1–21 (the hoarfrost mistaken
for snow), where the secondary term of the simile, the
vehicle alone, fills no fewer than fifteen lines in one
continuous sentence. Yet this is not, in spite of its
length, an unusually interesting example. More significant syntactically is a later one, that of the madness
of Athamas and Hecuba in *Inferno,* XXX, 1–21. In
cases of extreme elaboration, such as the last two
examples just mentioned, the critics have felt inclined
to point out their literary and rhetorical qualities.
Sapegno, for instance, has aptly remarked that the
sketch of the peasant who, mistaking the hoarfrost for
snow, "beats his thigh, to and fro complains, like a
starved wretch who knows not what to do," is, as
Sapegno would have it, "neither portrayed from life
nor psychologically developed in depth, but stylized
after a linear and gothic-like pattern of draftsmanlike
gracefulness"; Sapegno then goes on to indicate the
precious figures of speech employed there, such as
equivocal rhymes and so forth.[9]

If we move on from such similes or narrative passages unusually fraught with complex cultural sug-
gestions (let us think in passing of *Inferno* XIII) to
the "simplest" ones in the *Commedia,* the temptation
will be strong to assume, along with the Romantic
critics, that here, at last, we are graced with plain,

9. Dante Alighieri, *La Divina Commedia,* ed. N. Sapegno (Florence, 1955–57), *1,* 267–68. Applewhite, pp.
302–04, discusses Sapegno's remarks on this simile to support his case for the need to read the images contextually
in an even broader sense than that of their immediate function toward the narrative surrounding it. There will be
more on this later.

unalloyed, uncomplicated lyrical inspiration, the pure poetry we feel entitled to expect of a great poet in his best moments. However, a closer look will lead us to question the Romantic postulate of an absolute purity in the image—absolute in the sense of an expression of spontaneous, "naïve" inner experience unrelated to the poet's rhetorical and cultural baggage.

Let us take one simile which, in a poem so extraordinarily rich in imagery of all sorts and on all levels, could very well be given as the most telling single example of Dante's lyrical powers and perhaps his most beautiful single image—if such a choice does not sound foolhardy:[10]

> As in a serene night of full moon Trivia smiles among the eternal nymphs who paint the sky in every corner.

> (Quale ne' plenilunii sereni
>   Trivïa ride tra le ninfe etterne
>   che dipingon lo ciel per tutti i seni.)[11]
>   (*Paradiso,* XXIII, 25–27)

10. Eliot claimed that the *Commedia* is short in metaphor, especially in proportion with the similes ("Dante," p. 206), and has been taken to task for it (see n. 7). True enough, he had particularly in mind a comparison with Shakespeare, and in this sense his statement remains valid, but in absolute terms he was inaccurate, especially since he neglected to compare the three cantiche, which, as Miss Brandeis has shown, present strikingly different characteristics in this respect.

11. Following some of his characteristic remarks to the effect that in the *Paradiso* lyrical sketches and comparisons are worth more than the abstract representations of the blessed (including Christ "as a sun"), B. Croce concluded that, after all that abstract intellectualism, the dream of a

We can begin by summarizing the results of dozens of commentators.[12]

Comparetti first called attention to this image for its authentic sense of the ancient, in a way unknown to the Middle Ages. Of course, the moon often occurs in classical poetry and especially in Horace, for example, *Carmen saeculare,* ll. 35–36: "Siderum regina bicornis, audi,/Luna, puellas," and more pertinently, ll. 1–2: "Phoebe silvarumque potens Diana,/lucidum coeli decus, o colendi/semper et culti" (where *decus,* according to the interpreters, refers to Diana alone); similarly in *Epod.* XV, 1–2: "Coelo fulgebat Luna sereno/inter minora sidera."[13] The myth, at any rate, is perfectly fused in the representation, with a striking result of

---

mysterious and sacred beauty is at last suddenly thrust upon our minds by that accompanying comparison of Trivia (*La poesie di Dante,* pp. 143–45).

12. See, in particular, D. Comparetti, *Virgilio nel Medioevo* (Florence, 1937–41), *1,* 267–68; F. Pellegrini, *"Paradiso* XXIII," *Lectura Dantis,* Orsanmichele (Florence, 1904), p. 14; E. Trucchi, *Esposizione della Divina Commedia di Dante Alighieri* (3 vols. Milan, 1943), *3,* 377; M. Porena, *La mia Lectura Dantis* (Naples, 1932), pp. 341 ff.; Venturi, *Le similitudini dantesche ordinate;* Sacchetto, *Il gioco,* pp. 82–84; M. Apollonio, *Dante, Storia della* Commedia (Milan, 1951), 2, 857–61; Batard, *Dante, Minerve et Apollon,* pp. 448–50; Croce, *La poesie di Dante,* p. 145; M. Fubini, *Metrica e Poesia, Lezioni sulle forme metriche italiane.* I. *Dal 200 al Petrarca* (Milan, 1962), p. 21; Auerbach, *Dante,* p. 156 (on the image within its context); and, of the annotated editions of the poem, especially those by Scartazzini —Vandelli, Casini—Barbi, Torraca, Grabher, Porena, Momigliano, and, most conclusive in this respect, Sapegno. Quotations not further identified in the text refer to pages as indicated in this note, under the respective authors.

13. Also cf. *Aeneid,* VI, 13 and 35; VII, 516 and 774; *Metamorphoses,* II, 416, etc. Venturi also recalled Ecclesiasti-

naturalness. We have then learned classical reminiscences and classical beauty and tone. Yet Dante's
moon is quite another thing; its haunting quality is
Dante's own. This quality lies first in the phonetic
merits of those *e*'s and *i*'s, happily contrasting with the
dark, nocturnal *u* of "plenilunii"; we are reminded of
Francesca's "Ma se a conoscer la prima radice / . . . /
dirò come colui che piange e dice," where the palatal
vowels *e* and *i* conspire with the palatal consonants
c, g, and *sc,* as compared with Ugolino's "Ma se le mie
parole esser dien seme/che frutti infamia al traditor
ch'i' rodo,/parlare e lacrimar vedrai inseme," harsh
with the insistent *r*'s and *a*'s and the strongly iambic
rhythm.[14] If the vowels already predominate, they are
made even weightier by the two diaereses of "pleni-

---

cus L, 6: "Quasi stella matutina in medio nebulae et/quasi
luna plena in diebus suis lucet."

It might be added in passing that the Trivia (for Hecate-
Diane) of *Aeneid,* VI, 13 ("Iam subeunt Triviae lucos atque
aurea tecta") was interpreted in the humanism of Chartres
to refer to the trivium of the liberal arts: Aeneas and his
companions, after landing near Cumae, pass through a grove
sacred to Hecate, in search of Apollo's temple and the
Sibyl's cave, all this meaning that knowledge and wisdom
are reached through the preliminary curriculum of trivium
and quadrivium. See *Commentum Bernardi Silvestris super
sex libros Eneidos,* ed. W. Riedel (Gryphiswaldae, 1924).

14. Stress on phonetic analysis characterized the commentaries of Torraca and Grabher; M. Barbi warns against
the dangers inherent in the excessive use of this approach
in "Per un nuovo commento della *Divina Commedia,*"
Studi Danteschi, 19 (1935), p. 35, reprinted in Barbi, *Con
Dante e i suoi interpreti* (Florence, 1941). Enrico Thovez
went even farther in voicing the Italian critics' unwillingness
to stress sound as such in poetic language (alliteration, for
example, is probably rarer in Italian poetry than in any
other Latin, Romance, or Germanic language, and musicality

lunii" and "Trivïa," with the accompanying effect of
lengthening or rather slowing down the rhythm of
the two lines (the first of which is, physically speaking,
unusually short), so that the description is marked by
the static calm of a contemplative mood.

It will be recalled that the first term of the comparison is the apparition of Christ triumphant. The

---

per se is frequently looked down upon as an artistic merit);
as Fubini reminds us (*Metrica e Poesia*):

> Thovez, che ebbe a disdegno la poesia italiana, perché a
> suo parere troppo letteraria, uscí a dire che anche Dante
> era un letterato e che la bellezza di questa terzina era
> tutto un gioco fonico. In realtà le vocali qui non sono
> frutto di una ricerca esteriore di suoni, ma una cosa
> sola con la poesia, con le immagini suggerite da quelle
> denominazioni mitologiche: *Trivia, ninfe;* e tuttavia
> non sono qui solo per la delicata immagine che evocano,
> ma anche per il loro suono che . . . acquista un singolare
> rilievo. Osserviamo già nella parola *plenilunii* l'accenno
> a due colori dell'immagine: nella prima parte della
> parola il suono chiaro dell'*e* e nella seconda quello
> cupo dell'*u;* poi si fa più insistente il suono dell'*e*
> (*sereni*), ma già nella parola *plenilunii* con l'insistenza
> sulla vocale finale è accennato il suono dell'*i* che squilla
> nel verso seguente: *Trivia, ride, ninfe;* notiamo inol-
> tre l'allitterazione della *r* che domina con le *i* nel secon-
> do verso (ma si annuncia già nel primo con *sereni*),
> mentre nel primo verso domina la *l* con la *n.* Quindi
> riprende l'*e* (*etterne*), poi l'*i* (*dipingon*), ancora l'*e*
> (*ciel*) e infine ritorna il motivo in sordina dell'*u.* Questi
> suoni si combinano in mirabile armonia, e quello dell'*u,*
> tenuto come in sordina, ci suggerisce l'oscurità della
> notte, nella quale si diffonde l'azzurro notturno (suono
> dell'*e*), e gli *i* che tanto risaltano in questi versi ci danno
> quasi lo squillare di quella luce: abbiamo così una
> completa rappresentazione del paesaggio lunare.

(Not that the vowels have a color, as for Rimbaud, but they
acquire it in their encounter with other sounds and in the
general rhythm.)

This seems the best and most elaborate analysis of this
aspect of the simile. These remarks were prefaced with the

reader has been made aware of some imminent extraordinary spectacle from the beginning of the canto, first because of Beatrice fixedly looking to the horizon, like the bird eagerly awaiting the break of day ("Come l'augello, intra l'amate fronde"), then by her own high-sounding announcement of ll. 19–21. The description of Christ's triumph is indeed introduced by the Trivia simile, upon which follows the terzina

> over a myriad lamps preëminent
> I saw one sun which kindled each and all,
> as light from our sun to the stars is lent.
>   [Binyon's trans.]

(vidi sopra migliaia di lucerne
   un sol che tutte quante l'accendea,
   come fa il nostro le viste superne.)

Miss Batard points out the formal symmetry between the vehicle and tenor of the comparison—"migliaia" occupies a parallel position to "plenilunii," as does "sol" with respect to "Trivïa."[15]

---

warning that only by abstraction can we separate the visual from the phonetic aspects of such an image as this.

On metrical aspects of the *Comedy* and, in particular, on the diaereses, see E. Ciafardini, "Dieresi e sineresi nella *Divina Commedia*," *Rivista d'Italia*, *13* (1910), 888–919; F. D'Ovidio, *Versificazione italiana e arte poetica medievale* (Milan, 1910), reprinted in D'Ovidio, *Versificazione romanza: Poetica e poesia medievale* (3 vols. Naples, 1932), *1*, 9–61 on diaeresis. Both give our simile as an example of diaeresis.

15. The remainder of Miss Batard's analysis is worth quoting:

> L'impression de sérénité y naît plutôt de la musique que des lignes descriptives; et l'allégresse vient du rire de Diane.... Ce rire demeure un rire pour les yeux, une

However, something is still obviously missing if we are to catch a little more of the ineffable secret of this powerful image. Without presuming to provide the final key to the aesthetic mystery, we may, by further analysis, get closer to the manifold meaning and uncover some of the raw materials of which the poet availed himself in exercising his choice of expressive means.

From the metrical point of view one finds little that appears peculiar in these verses. The secondary term of the simile presents the pattern: 1 **6 10**; 1 **4 8 10**; 3 **6** 8 **10**.[16] Indeed, the rhythm of this terzina is made of a subtle melody that depends on semantic ties and syntax rather than on the metrical structure *stricto sensu*.

The following terzina perhaps can offer a little help in our difficult search for a fleeting rhythm:

> peinture lumineuse (*dipingon*), en même temps qu'il s'égrène en voyelles légères, en succession de liquides, de dentales et d'i, dont la vibration aigüe alterne avec l'éclat atténué des o et des e, appuyés sur des nasales et des gutturales . . . pour rebondir, au troisième [vers] en une vague unique, large comme le ciel qu'elle recouvre . . . immense et souriant nocturne. (p. 449)

But for an example of more complete symmetry in a simile, see *Inferno,* II, 127–32 ("Quali i fioretti, dal notturno gelo"), and Applewhite's sensitive remarks, pp. 300–01.

16. Another pattern interestingly close to this can be found in the simile of *Paradiso,* XXVII, 67–69, at least in the first and third lines and in the ligature between the end of the second and the following. The comparison, however, will show how little the external rhythm per se might count. More pertinent is the similarity of rhythm in the third line of the simile in *Paradiso,* XXVI, 85–87: "Come la fronda che flette la cima/nel transito del vento, e poi si leva/per la propria virtú che la sublíma."

La gloria di colui che tutto move
per l'universo penetra e risplende
in una parte più e meno altrove.

(*Paradiso*, I, 1–3)

The similarity of the third lines goes beyond the pattern of stresses; we find in both a dynamic, triumphant tone of contemplated discovery enhanced by a mild enjambment. This enjambment is quite clear in the second case ("e risplende in una parte più"), especially with that caesura after "penetra." It is less clear in the Trivia terzina, and yet there is also some ligature there between the second and third lines, a melodic and semantic tie even more than properly syntactical, since "ninfe" is not self-explanatory ("stelle" would have been) and requires the "che dipingon lo ciel" which follows to complete itself. Some critics have found in that "nymphs" for "stars" a reference to *Purgatorio,* XXXI, 106, which would explain the term at this point, not as a bold mythological metaphor, but as a theological reminiscence for which the ground had been explicitly prepared. This is, however, an evident misreading of the previous passage ("Noi siam qui ninfe, e nel ciel siamo stelle"), where the angelic intelligences of the four stars embodying the cardinal virtues (not *all* the stars) appeared to Dante as allegorical nymphs in the retinue of Beatrice's chariot—the same four stars contemplated in *Purgatorio,* I, 23, 37, and VIII, 91.[17]

17. For this misinterpretation cf., in particular, Trucchi, *Esposizione,* p. 377, and Porena's commentary to the *Comedy,* where it is discussed and rejected. Porena found *ninfe* a "strange denomination" for stars, which *Purgatorio,* XXXI, 106 would not suffice to justify.

The nymphs of the simile have no part in the allegory of the poem; they are only recalled by Trivia in a bold transposition from earth to sky—as Diana is accompanied on earth by a train of nymphs, so has Diana-Luna her retinue of stars.

The active, dynamic quality of the key terms, "ride" and "dipingon," after the still-life calm of the first line contributes to that vividness and clarity of representation which for Tasso put Dante almost on a par with Homer, specifically referring to the quality of imagination which he called "chiarezza," thus translating the Greek *enárgheia* and Cicero's rendition of it, *evidentia*.[18] Those two key words attracted attention, as witnessed by at least two cases of reminiscence that

---

18. W. P. Ker, "Divina Commedia," in *Collected Essays,* ed. Ch. Whibley (London, 1925), *1,* 305–20, acutely pointed out Tasso's judgment while discussing Dante's similes: "Dante was the first modern poet to use with full consciousness of its value the epic simile, and his similes are Homeric in their fulness, clearness, and security" (p. 310). The distinguished critic, however, was paraphrasing his source rather freely. Tasso's rendition of the Greek ἐνάργεια fluctuates a bit vaguely among *energia, chiarezza, evidenza,* and even *espressione:* Ker's "fulness" seems to refer to Tasso's "diligentissima narrazione," and "security" to "ardire." Cf. "Discorsi dell'Arte Poetica," *3* (in T. Tasso, *Prose,* ed. E. Mazzali [Milan-Naples, 1959], p. 401): "Stando che lo stile sia un instrumento co'l quale imita il poeta quelle cose che d'imitare si ha proposte, necessaria è in lui l'energia: la quale sì con parole pone innanzi a gli occhi la cosa che pare altrui non di udirla, ma di vederla"; and "Discorsi del Poema Eroico," *6* (ibid., pp. 709–10): "Ed oltre tutte cose è in lei richiesta quella probabilità e quella che da' Latini è detta *evidentia,* da' Greci *energia;* da noi si direbbe *chiarezza* o *espressione* non men propriamente; ma è quella virtù che ci fa quasi veder le cose che si narrano, la quale nasce da una diligentissima narrazione, come si vede ne le narrazioni del conte Ugolino: *La bocca sollevò* etc.; e ne l'altre cose ch'ivi

one could choose at random: Fazio degli Uberti:
"Come per primavera, avanti 'l giorno,/ride Diana
nell'aire serena/d'una luce sì piena,/che par che ne
risplenda tutto 'l cielo," and Poliziano of Venus: "di
quella dea che 'l terzo ciel dipinge."[19]

The association of light and smile was a common
one, especially within the Platonic tradition: a luminous body seems to smile, and a smiling creature gives
forth light. As Ficino later puts it: "What is God's
light? . . . What is it in the celestial things? It is . . . a
smile of heaven."[20] More specifically, with an interesting physiological application, Dante himself said:

> Because of the glad nature whence it grows
> The mingled virtue through the body beams
> As gladness through the living pupil shows.
>
> [Binyon's trans.]

> (Per la natura lieta onde deriva,
> la virtù mista per lo corpo luce
> come letizia per pupilla viva.)
>
> (*Paradiso*, II, 142–44)

son narrate. E quella comparazione ancora è piena di grande
evidenza: *Come le pecorelle escon dal chiuso* etc." And finally
(ibid., p. 715): "Dante è quasi terzo fra costoro [namely,
Homer and Virgil], come dice egli stesso, fra cotanto senno;
ed è più simile ad Omero ne l'ardire e ne la licenza e nel
mescolamento de le parole antiche e barbare ch'a Virgilio;
ed il somiglia ancora in quella che da' Latini è stata detta
evidenzia."

19. Both examples were quoted by Venturi, *Le similitudini dantesche ordinate.* See Fazio degli Uberti, *Il Ditta-
mondo e le Rime,* ed. G. Corsi (Bari, 1952), 2, 8 (*Rime,* 3);
A. Poliziano, *Stanze,* ed. V. Pernicone (Turin, 1954), I, i, 4.

20. M. Ficino, *De lumine* in *Opera Omnia* (Turin, 1959,
reprinted 1962), *1*, 978: "Quid lux in Deo? . . . Quid in

The luminosity of a body is the shining forth of an inner joy, an active and live spirituality, just as the visible smile that is expressed in the natural light of an eye's pupil is a reflection of that joie de vivre which it derives from the perfect happiness of the Godhead, its Creator. Thus we have a sort of triple equation between spiritual divine happiness, physical light, and smiling.[21] Indeed, God Himself, Neoplatonically re-

---

angelis? Quid in coelestibus? Copia vitae ab angelis, virtutis explicatio a coelo, risus coeli."

21. The explicit association of light and smile is rather common in Dante, and it is first applied to celestial bodies in *Purgatorio*, I, 19–20: "Lo bel pianeta che d'amar conforta/ faceva tutto rider l'orïente." Smile and burning flame together are also associated with love, as in *Paradiso*, XX, 13–14: "O dolce amor che di riso t'ammanti,/quanto parevi ardente in que' flailli!" Also cf. *Paradiso*, XXVII, 4; XXVIII, 83; XXIX, 7 ("riso dell'universo," "il ciel ne ride," "col volto di riso dipinto").

In the wake of ancient and medieval light-metaphysics, poets had long been on their mettle to give eloquent and elaborate expression to their fascination with the all-pervasive power and meaning of light in all its manifestations. If, for instance, Dante's "E vidi *lume* in forma di rivera/*fluvido di fulgore*" (*Paradiso*, XXX, 61–62) strikes us with its magnificent, almost "baroque" redundance, the possible sources usually mentioned by the commentators (Ps. XXV:9–10, and XLV:5; Dan. VII:10; Rev. XXII:1) may do little to give us a clue to its formal, verbal inspiration, but a medieval poet like Alcuin may go a long way with his: "Illic invenies veterum vestigia patrum . . . Africa lucifluo vel quidquid lumine sparsit," where *lucifluo lumine* corresponds exactly to "lume fluvido di fulgore": Alcuin, "Versus de . . . sanctis euboricensis ecclesiae," in *Poetae Latini Aevi Carolini,* ed. E. Dümmler, M. G. H. (Berlin, 1881), *1,* 203.

On certain aspects of Dante's light-, color-, and flower-imagery see the fine observations of G. Getto, *Aspetti della Poesia di Dante* (Florence, 1947), pp. 141–49 and, more extensively, in a direction of intellectual derivations, J. A. Mazzeo, *Structure and Thought in the Paradiso* (Ithaca, ferred to by Dante as light in his final definition of the Godhead, also smiles to His creation ("arridi").[22]

Trivia was undoubtedly more alive, more human than Luna, and Dante did well to avail himself of a mythological personification, but she truly comes alive through her laugh, in a sublime anthropomorphic touch that takes us away on the wings of fancy. Yet such human attributes for the behavior of inanimate beings and spectacles were not only poetic common-places, but widespread rhetorical ones. "The meadow laughs" (*pratum ridet*) was an old school example of μεταφορά (*translatio,* transfer) as the basic rhetorical figure, as seen in Quintilian, VIII, 2, 6.[23] It will suffice

---

1958), Chap. 6, and *Medieval Cultural Tradition in Dante's* Comedy (Ithaca, 1960), Chaps. 2, 3.

22.   O luce etterna che sola in te sidi,
        sola t'intendi, e da te intelletta
        e intendente te ami e arridi!
                (*Paradiso,* XXXIII, 124–26)

The terzina is a celebrated and masterly synthesis of the three main philosophical and theological currents of medieval thought—the Platonic or, more precisely, Neoplatonic in the first line, the Aristotelian in the second, and the Augustinian-Christian in the "ami" of the third. This is also one argument against the unilateral interpretation of Dante as a Thomist to the exclusion of other trends, and in support of his splendid eclecticism.

23. See E. R. Curtius, *European Literature and Latin Middle Ages* (New York, Harper Torchbooks, 1963), p. 128. Incidentally, in dealing with "personal" metaphors Curtius (p. 132) gives several examples from Dante, but not the most important and unusual of Lady Poverty, "bride" of Christ, and of St. Francis (which Momigliano considered "a character, more than a personification": see his annotated edition of the *Divine Comedy* [Florence, 1952], at *Paradiso,* XI, 67–69), or that of the stars as "nymphs," which somehow appear as the Moon's "maids."

ALDO SCAGLIONE

here to recall "il rider dell'erbe" of *Paradiso,* XXX, 77.
But since we are in heaven among the stars, we may
recall that a strong and specific suggestion came directly from astrology, since the stars that laughed in
their mansions were common stock of the necromantic
literature, whether that expression of vitality was seen
as a benevolent smiling on the universe and its human
denizens (whence the expression, "fortune smiles on
someone," since the goddess Fortuna was also a celestial intelligence, a quasi-star herself) or as a wicked
and ill-foreboding chuckle. The latter possibility was
the expression of a deep-seated sense of the irrational,
the evil hidden in a mysterious Nature, which the medieval need for a stable, static, and rational ordering
of the universe tended to reject together with the
damnable black magic. Deep in the medieval man
there lay an instinct that compelled him to attribute
life and soul to every part of the universe, to humanize
it, and the astrological view of astral influences on our
destinies tended not to dehumanize man by making
him a part of a purely physical nature—which was
reserved to the post-Galilean celestial mechanic—but
rather to make the whole world anthropomorphic.
The stars or their "minds" rule over men, but "the sage
will overcome the stars," the manuals of astrology kept
repeating.[24] Of course, Dante places himself beyond
the letter and the spirit of these traditions in that his
Trivia is engaged in a spectacle of pure aesthetic beauty

24. See E. Garin, *Medioevo e Rinascimento* (Florence,
1954), pp. 159–62. Garin refers to the pseudo-Platonic
Liber vaccae, the *Picatrix,* perhaps the most important manual
of magic art in the Middle Ages, and Albumasar's *Introduc-
torium,* the source of Ibn Ezra, from whom derived Peter of

rather than in feeling satisfaction about the success
of any occult practices on her part or on that of any
other beings or intelligences. Yet, at least part of the
literal ingredients may have been suggested from
those astrologic quarters.

The nymphs, in their turn, are engaged in the act
of "painting" the sky, a kind of artistic activity of
their own. At this point, however, the smiling of
Trivia is communicated to all her nymphs, for it is the
whole, vast celestial painting that is alive with smiling,
and we cannot help but be reminded of the sheets of
parchment that smile after being brought to life by
the great illuminator Franco Bolognese:

> "Art thou not Oderisi," then said I,
>   "Honour of Gubbio, honour of that art,
>   The illuminators famed in Paris ply?"
> "Brother, the pages smile more on the mart
>   Which Franco of Bologna paints," said he:
>   "Now the honour is all his, mine only in part."
>   [Binyon's trans.]

> ("Oh!" diss'io lui, "non se' tu Oderisi,
>   l'onor d'Agobbio e l'onor di quell'arte
>   ch'alluminar chiamata è in Parisi?"
> "Frate," diss'elli "più ridon le carte
>   che pennelleggia Franco bolognese:
>   l'onore è tutto or suo, e mio in parte.")
>   (*Purgatorio,* XI, 79–84)

Abano (1257–1315?). Garin uses the Trivia image to illustrate: "E mentre l'astrologo al di là delle incorruttibili stelle
vede Trivia ridere fra le ninfe eterne per la gioia della sua
dimora, il mago ascolta le forze che agitano l'intimo degli
esseri."

The painting that laughs is a Dantesque image. But what kind of metaphor is this? Obviously, "dipingon" cannot be called to the poet's imagination by the subject "ninfe": nymphs don't usually paint. First, although strongly individual in Dante, this bold metaphor echoes the traditional analogy between flowers (nature's colors, wherewith she paints her meadows) and stars: "et flores pro stellis, et stellae sideraque pro floribus ponuntur."[25] Calderón later called the stars "flowers of the night," as, vice versa, the flowers are "stars of the day"; now the sky is "a field of stars"; now a field is "a sky of flowers."[26]

"Ride" placed the image on a human level, while the visual flash of that smile showed the triumph of an aesthetic beauty; "dipingon" momentarily transposes the experience to the visual plane of the figurative arts.[27] "Dipingon" also presents a rather curious effect

25. G. J. Vossius, *Commentariorum rhetoricorum sive Oratoriarum Institutionum Libri Sex* (4th ed. Leyden, 1643), Bk. IV, Chap. 6, p. 89, where he deals with reciprocal metaphors, with examples from several authors.
26. L. Spitzer, *Literaturblatt für germ. und rom. Philologie,* 46 (1925), 105, referring to Lindner, *Die poetische Personifikation in den Jugendschauspielen Calderons,* p. 52. This example is related by B. Migliorini, *Saggi linguistici* (Florence, 1957), p. 23, as reciprocal metaphor (which would hark back to Aristotle, *Poetics,* XXI) of the type *velorum pandimus alas, nare per aestatem liquidam,* hence *mare velivolum* (Servius, *In Vergilii Carmina Commentarii*).
27. This "artisan" touch should not surprise us, since it is only one step removed from the favorite book metaphors and imagery from writing that Curtius so masterfully described (*European Literature,* pp. 302–47). Dante naturally visualizes the sky as a picture and a place for colorful painting: let us recall that God himself "painted" the Eagle in Jupiter (*Paradiso,* XVIII, 109). See more examples in L. Malagoli, *Linguaggio e poesia nella D.C.* (Genoa, 1949), p. 23.

of indirect synesthesia in that the rhythm of the line, rather than its semantic value, carries a suggestion of dance-like movement. In reading the last half of the simile, "le ninfe etterne/che dipingon lo ciel per tutti i seni," we feel a change of rhythmic pattern coming; after the slow and weighty first two lines we have a quickening of pace, and we rush through the third line without any sensible stress before the ictus of the sixth syllable ("ciel"). On the strength of that sweeping dynamic movement of quasi-enjambment, we get a vague but subtly effective suggestion of a moonlit caroling of ethereal nymphs.

So much for "dipingon," but let us once again notice in passing the extraordinary concentration of metaphoric images—ridere, ninfe, dipingere—and think not too unkindly of Eliot's finding Dante poor in metaphors! The stars, then, are colors, like flowers, and as such laugh, like Franco's painted colors, and, by the artistic hand of God, paint the sky. But they are more human than that; they are (colorful) nymphs. "Ride," referring specifically to Trivia, extends its graces implicitly and poetically to the nymphs who form her royal cortege.

What now of "seni"? It has been said that this word adds dimension by hinting the vastness of an open sky.[28] Yet "seni" (corners) is quite limiting; it makes the spectacle a rather familiar one, bringing it down

28. Batard, *Dante, Minerve et Apollon,* p. 449; more specifically, Malagoli, p. 89, where the whole image is given as an example of "la spazialità dantesca," while "sanza veder principio di fulgori" of l. 84 is said to add "infinity" to its context. I agree with this second remark, whereas I find that the first needs qualification.

to human proportions. I prefer to recall Courthope's remarks on the difference between Milton's unlimited spaces and Dante's finite ones.[29] The vastness is suggested by the sweeping rhythm of the line, but there is, in the localization by "seni," something that sets the spectator at ease in this immensity, rather than filling him with disquieting awe.

We have attempted to see how the image works from within, in a capillary way. However, more important and more typical of Dante's way of composing is the value of the image in its context. We have used a microscopic approach as a starting point. The remainder of this analysis will show, I hope, the reason for such insistence on a very small portion of a canto, since the three lines discussed turn out to be the central ones in a pattern of imagery covering the whole canto, which cannot be properly understood without appreciating the fine and discreet texture of its allusive figurative language.

The question of the interaction of Dante's imagery, especially within each episode or canto, is an important one that has been sadly neglected. A young critic has recently raised it and pointed out a few rather scattered and timid precedents in the work of the English critic W. J. Courthope, Irma Brandeis, and Yvonne Batard.[30]

Courthope seems to have been first in asserting that Dante's imagery must be appreciated within the con-

29. W. J. Courthope, "A Consideration of Macaulay's Comparison of Dante and Milton," *Proceedings of the British Academy,* 3 (London, 1907–08), 259–74.

30. Applewhite, "Dante's Use of the Extended Simile," pp. 295–96. The other titles are cited in n. 6 and n. 29 above.

text of the poem as adding to it and deriving from it meaning and value; the quality of the images is more than visual, and they bear "relation to the principal poetic device of the poem." He writes:

> in spite of the great distinctness of imagery in the *Divine Comedy,* it is a mistake to suppose, with Macaulay, that the distinctness is employed "simply to make the meaning of the writer as clear to the reader as it is to himself." It is employed really because the whole atmosphere of Dante's poem is allegorical; because objects of sense have within him a spiritual meaning, which can be fully grasped only by a process of reason and reflection.[31]

Macaulay's error and Courthope's rebuttal were characteristically repeated respectively by Eliot and his critics, such as Thomas A. FitzGerald and Irma Brandeis. For Eliot, in FitzGerald's words, the similes' "purpose is solely to make us *see more definitely* the scene which Dante put before us in the preceding lines." For the sake of fairness, Eliot is here somehow misquoted, since he was actually speaking of one particular simile found in *Inferno,* XV, 21, where the generalization is not clearly implied, and where the reference to the *preceding lines* does not mean that Dante usually followed the tenor with the vehicle, only that in this case he did. Applewhite repeats these two charges without correcting them.[32]

31. Courthope, pp. 266–67.
32. See titles and pages in n. 7 above. See also M. Praz, "T. S. Eliot e Dante," in *Machiavelli in Inghilterra ed altri*

In a string of crisply worded and subtly articulated distinctions, Miss Brandeis claims that the three *cantiche* differ in the use of imagery—a point particularly well taken. Metaphors are few in the *Inferno,* and similes are mostly designed to enhance visual qualities; in the *Purgatorio* metaphors proliferate and "add to what you see" a symbolic insight into the meaning of visions; and in the *Paradiso* the "discourse glitters with metaphors that say nothing of any visible scene whatever," since the poet "has passed the symbolic as well as the literal masks, and finally has come to rest, simply and immediately, upon essential being." Furthermore, this sensitive critic calls attention to the fact that each image is not complete in itself, but extends its value and import to the surrounding context.

If this strikes the student as the soundest and most sensible approach, it must be added that the idea is not entirely new, although it has never been formulated so methodically and so broadly. F. Olivero, for example, dedicated a chapter of his study of Dante's imagery to the linking and continuation of the metaphorical images,[33] and on the level of practical criticism, certain obvious cases in which an episode or canto is geared to recurring motifs in its imagery have been pointed out innumerable times and analyzed accordingly; suffice it to mention the examples of the imagery

---

Saggi (2d ed. Rome, 1943), pp. 239–67; this is especially interesting with regard to Eliot's dependence on Ezra Pound for many elements of his approach to Dante's poetic forms and style.

33. See n. 6 above, pp. 63–72 of Ital. ed. (1940), pp. 53–62 of Eng. ed. (1936).

of birds in the episode of Francesca da Rimini and the rhetorico-précieux stylistic imitation in that of Pier delle Vigne.[34]

Nevertheless, no one seems to have applied this sensible method of analysis and interpretation to the very canto that seems written for it, Canto XXIII of *Paradiso*. Most critics agree that it is one of the most beautiful of the entire *Commedia*.[35] They justly underline its lyrical purity in that the imagery seems to take over completely and brush narration and even dialogue to a marginal position. But in their detailed analyses they do not go beyond the values of the individual images and single impressions, as if a great canto could be made by a loose string of powerful strokes of the imagination.

Since we have started by centering our attention on the simile of the moon—for that seems to be a sort of center of the canto's lyrical imagery—let us now extend our analysis by moving on from that point into the surrounding context. The most immediate context

34. Applewhite's keen analysis is also restricted to the *Inferno*. As a particularly significant analysis along the lines indicated see, apropos of Pier delle Vigne's episode, L. Spitzer, "Speech and Language in *Inf.* XIII," *Romanische Literaturstudien 1936–1956* (Tübingen, 1959), pp. 544–68.

35. R. Montano, "La Poesia di Dante, III: Il Paradiso," *Delta*, 20–21 (1959), esp. pp. 66–75, calls this the most beautiful canto of the *Commedia*. See esp. L. Tonelli, "Il Canto XXIII del *Paradiso*," *Convivium*, 5 (1932), 675–91. Tonelli finds the fundamental inspiration of the canto in the compenetration of the natural and the spiritual, the human and the transcendental, and repeats Tommaseo's summary of its motifs: "This Canto smiles with the images of light and flowers, harmony and angels, motherly love and child's innocence. To harmony, light, and motherhood appropriately correspond angels, flowers, and children" (p. 685).

is the primary term of the simile itself, which has not yet attracted our attention. Miss Batard states that one should choose the Trivia simile as an example of supreme achievement in the poem because of a number of virtues, including "l'équilibre des deux termes comparés."[36] We could hardly agree. If all the critic means here is the symmetry between the sound and position of "plenilunii" and "migliaia" on the one hand, and "Trivïa" and "sol" on the other, we can only say that we would expect more than that from a poet of Dante's stature. The fact is that one of the striking features of this passage is precisely the lack of equilibrium between vehicle and tenor.[37] The reader cannot help but notice that the simile is so powerfully absorbing that it sways his attention from the very event which, according to the normal function of such a figure of speech, it was supposed to aid (especially if we take Eliot's attitude).

In terms of relationship with the context, then, we are in for a surprise at first. Indeed, the vehicle and tenor lack even a logical relationship. The pilgrim is dazzled by the light of the heavenly militia, over which shines the infinitely more intense light of Christ. It would not be fitting, in terms of the figure, to compare this spectacle with that of a starry sky dominated by a full moon[38]—all the more so if we consider that Christ

36. Batard, *Dante, Minerve et Apollon,* p. 449.
37. We would do better to turn elsewhere in the poem for an example of harmony between primary and secondary terms of a comparison. I would begin by pointing out, for instance, *Paradiso,* XII, 10–27 (the synchronized dancing and singing of the two crowns of theologians in the Sun compared to a double rainbow and the myth of Echo).
38. Cf. Porena, *La mia Lectura Dantis,* p. 362.

is metaphorically called, in the tenor, "un sol" which spreads its light among the soul-stars (lucerne), just as the physical sun lights up (accende) stars and planets, "come fa il nostro le viste superne," a function which clearly does not befit the moon.[39] Nor does the plenitude of light of the paradisiacal vision resemble the prevalence of dark emptiness in the night sky, even if it is starry and there is a full moon. But the function of the figure is neither scientific nor descriptively, sensorially realistic; it is purely emotional, and as such not only successful, but among the most "convincing" in the poem. Indeed, that ecstatic vision of nocturnal beatitude passes from our eyes and ears into our hearts, and we feel that moonlit heaven within us.[40]

The failure to realize this fundamental truth about Dante's imagery is the gravest fault of Macaulay's, Eliot's, and many other critics' insistence on the reality of the vision and its representation, hence, on the visual character of the imagery as aid and support for the representation itself. This mistaken perspective has done injustice to the finer level of Dante's communication with the reader, which is not the objective level but the sentimental one, as has been admirably expressed, for

39. Medieval philosophers and astronomers shared this scientific error, according to which the stars did not shine with their own light. The misconception does nothing to help our simile. Also cf. *Paradiso,* XX, 4–6, and *Convivio,* II, xiii, 15. Christ was compared to sun, moon, and star in Rev. XXI:23 and XXII:16 ("lux quae illuminat omnem hominem venientem in hunc mundum").

40. "C'è una tale commozione estatica e mistica, tale una dolcezza d'immagini, e soprattutto tale una musica . . . che l'animo nostro . . . sente veramente diffondersi in sé come una beatifica inondazione di cielo" (Porena, p. 362).

instance, by Sapegno apropos of the Cross of Mars.[41] Similarly, for *Paradiso* XXIII, the critics have not looked hard enough beyond or rather beneath the surface of the truly but somehow misleading visual, "physical" beauty of the images per se; they have remained content with a vague and uncommitted definition of that mood that is discreetly communicated by the poet to the critically unconscious though deeply affected reader.

The logical discourse is overcome by the poetry of the artifact, which acts through intuitive rather than rational channels. The truth about the Trivia image is that it would not so effectively contribute to the establishment of that heavenly ecstasy which the poet intends to achieve at this point were it not because of that very lack of logic, that disproportion between the terms of comparison. The moon serves the poet better than any further confirmation of the sun-like quality of Christ's epiphany, because the feminine moon[42]

41. Si avverta tuttavia come Dante tende ad alleggerire e sfumare l'immagine, piuttosto che a materializzarla, a dar rilievo al sentimento più che alla figura, pur definita con geometrico rigore. Il linguaggio sottolinea il vago e l'indeterminato della visione ... le pause ... suscitano ... un complesso di valori analogici e sentimentali. ... La sensazione visiva si risolve ... nel fascino di una percezione indefinita, che è come il riflesso, spiritualizzato, dello spettacolo sensibile.

(Sapegno, annotated ed. of the *Divine Comedy,* n. to *Paradiso,* XIV, 128.)

42. We cannot afford here to overlook the feminine association of the Latin and Romance *Luna,* because, whatever its etymological justification, the linguistic form of the word is indissolubly espoused to the emotive awareness of the Latin speaker. For Germans it may be *der Mond* and *die Sonne,* but for the Latin speaker the moon *is* a woman.

belongs in the same texture with the rose, a feminine flower, under whose metaphor the Virgin Mary is hidden (v. 73)—mankind's loving Mother toward whom all the souls literally bend with longing by elongating themselves like flames moving with an upward thrust ("in su si stese con la sua fiamma"), just as a baby's arms will go toward the mother after he has fed at her breast, for the grateful love that kindles him even to this outward show,

> E come fantolin che 'nver la mamma
> tende le braccia, poi che 'l latte prese,
> per l'animo che 'nfin di fuor s'infiamma
>
> (ll. 121–23)

Not only is the Trivia image part of a larger unit, but it would not even sound such a deep note in the reader without its framework. Sapegno has pithily hinted at this aesthetic fact without attempting to define that framework.[43]

Our way of reading the imagery has now brought us to the verge of a final discovery. The canto is, truly enough, not only the triumph of Christ, but the triumph of Mary as well, or rather of both in the indivisible bond of Mother and Son. Yet, in a sense, it is more the triumph of Mary than of Christ.[44] This deep

43. "Del resto l'immagine dantesca deriva gran parte della sua vibrazione lirica dalla cornice, in cui si colloca, di commossa adorazione e di stupefatta gratitudine per la meraviglia e la grandezza dello spettacolo celeste" (Sapegno, annotated ed. of the *Divine Comedy,* n. to *Paradiso,* XXIII, 26).

44. Porena, *La mia Lectura Dantis,* p. 341 ff., does define *Paradiso* XXIII as the Canto of Mary, but without specifically

meaning of the canto is achieved more through the imagery than through the literal narration, for, as befits the moving homage to the Virgin, the canto's delicate melody starts out in a minor key with that

---

relying on the imagery or interpreting the Trivia passage in this light.

All in all, this canto has received comparatively limited attention from the critics. Paraphrastic expositions are contained in such works as Trucchi's *Esposizione* and Apollonio's *Dante,* and especially in the old but still valuable W. W. Vernon, *Readings on the Paradiso of Dante, Chiefly Based on the Commentary of Benvenuto da Imola, 2* (2d ed. London, 1909), Canto XXIII, pp. 224–49 (a competent mosaic of the more authoritative commentaries available to that date). Relevant specific "letture" of the canto have not been too numerous: the most competent is, perhaps, that of U. Cosmo, *L'Ultima Ascesa, Introduzione alla lettura del Paradiso* (Bari, 1936), pp. 293–310. Cosmo stresses the centrality of both Beatrice and Mary above even Christ, at least from the emotional viewpoint, but undertakes neither the establishment of a pattern of imagery nor the relation of the "two women's" reciprocal function. Dante's turning "with greater love and desire" toward Mary (and Beatrice) than toward Christ was explained, in his inspired, personal way, by A. Fogazzaro, "Il Canto del Trionfo di Cristo," *Nuova Antologia, 123* (1906), 177–89, on the basis of Dante's being "a mystic in love, a theologian in religion."

To the "letture" by F. Pellegrini, L. Tonelli, and R. Montano, add P. P. Trompeo's in G. Getto, ed., *Letture Dantesche, 3* (Florence, 1961), 469–80; A. Tomaselli, "Il trionfo di Cristo nel *Paradiso* di Dante," *Rivista d'Italia, 25* (1922), 396–410; Nicola Carinci, *Il Trionfo di Cristo e della Vergine nella Divina Commedia* (Lavagna, 1940); Emilio Santini, "Il Canto XXIII del *Paradiso,*" *Studi Danteschi, 32* (1954), 37–49 (containing, in particular, several sensitive observations on the functionality of a nonelegiac, nonaffective, transcendental, and epic representation of Christ— p. 41); Mario Casella, "Il Canto XXIII del *Paradiso,*" *Studi Danteschi, 33* (1955–56), 11–34; Sebastiano Lo Nigro, "Lettura del Canto XXIII del *Paradiso,*" *Siculorum Gymnasium,* N.S., 8 (1955), 223–40. In the recent bibliography *Gli Studi Danteschi dal 1950 al 1964* by E. Esposito (Rome,

arresting simile of the bird quietly and eagerly waiting
for the sun to appear:

> As the bird amidst the loved foliage who hath
> brooded on the nest of her sweet offspring through
> the night which hideth things from us,
> who, to look upon their longed-for aspect and
> to find the, food wherewith to feed them, wherein
> her heavy toils are pleasant to her,
> foreruns the time, upon the open spray, and
> with glowing love awaiteth the sun, fixedly gaz-
> ing for the dawn to rise.
> [Carlyle-Wicksteed trans.]

> (Come l'augello, intra l'amate fronde,
>   posato al nido de' suoi dolci nati
>   la notte che le cose ci nasconde,
> che, per veder li aspetti disiati
>   e per trovar lo cibo onde li pasca,

1965) I also find listed two studies which I have been unable
to see: Salvatore Gallo, "Dante araldo dell'Assunzione,"
Responsabilità del Sapere (Rome, 1951), pp. 39–59, and
Francesco Squarcia, *Il Canto XXIII del Paradiso* (Parma,
1955). See also, Hermann Gmelin's outstanding commentary: D. Alighieri, *Die Göttliche Komödie: Kommentar, 3*
(Stuttgart, 1957), 406–20. Gmelin perceptively stresses the
metaphorical and symbolic texture of the whole canto as
well as its division into the two perfectly balanced triumphs
of Christ and Mary, each occupying twenty-three terzine,
and each unfolding through parallel stages. See, finally,
Umberto Bosco's new, sensitive "lettura," *"Paradiso XXIII,"
Eighty-Third Annual Report of the Dante Society* (1965),
pp. 1–22.
   On Dante's attitude toward Christ, here and in general, cf.
K. Vossler, *Mediaeval Culture: An Introduction to Dante
and His Times,* trans. W. C. Lawton (New York, 1929), *1,*
209–14.

in che gravi labor li sono aggrati,
previene il tempo in su aperta frasca,
e con ardente affetto il sole aspetta,
fiso guardando pur che l'alba nasca.)

(ll. 1–9)

In a sort of subtle leitmotif, the pattern of the moon-Trivia echoes and extends that night, "la notte che le cose ci nasconde," in which the bird sits waiting on the top branches of the tree, while the sun is announced by the imminent dawn but is not yet there "il sole aspetta, /fiso guardando pur che l'alba nasca.")

The canto is all textured by the similes, which for once take the upper hand over the rich and numerous metaphors. There are ten similes in the canto, and they comprise, counting vehicles and tenors, about fifty of the one hundred and thirty-nine lines—an unusual proportion, and one of the highest in the *Commedia*.[45] But of those ten similes the four that stand out most forcefully transmit a sequence of imagery that goes from night—imminent daybreak—awaited sun ("Come l'augello, intra l'amate fronde"), to the moon in smiling triumph ("Quale ne' plenilunii sereni"), to a sunlit patch seen from the shadow ("Come a raggio di sol che puro mei"), and finally to the baby stretching his arms toward the mother ("E come fantolin che 'nver la mamma").

45. Venturi counted eleven similes here, including "scese una facella,/formata in cerchio a guisa di corona" (ll. 94–95). Even a quick glance at the useful index by cantos, which was added posthumously in the third edition of his *Le similitudini dantesche ordinate* (1911), reveals that very few cantos of the *Commedia* contain more or even as many similes as *Paradiso* XXIII.

This is the lyrical texture of this glorious canto;
this is the unitary pattern that underlies it, dominates
its meaning, and establishes its emotional value: a
lingering in the twilight; an eager, dynamic expectation of illumination; a sweet "romantic" touch of
melancholy yearning toward a total liberation from a
still prevailing darkness; a looking to the Holy Virgin
who with her unequaled motherly solicitude takes us
from that darkness to that light.[46] By overplaying the
"whirlpool of light" and the "symphony in clear tones"
which is only one side of this manifold spectacle, the
critics have done injustice to the whole, detracted from
its richness and variety, and overlooked the more
peculiar element in the atmosphere of the canto, namely, its distinctive chiaroscuro, literal and figurative.

So that Dante's eyes may not be blinded by His
brightness, Christ rises again to the Empyrean, and the
pilgrim beholds the fantastic spectacle of the army of
the blest illumined from above by the dazzling light of
Christ Himself, now out of sight. The chiaroscuro of

46. As to the relative "darkness" which is the starting
point of the movement toward the promised illumination,
we must not forget that the preceding canto ended on the
strong note of the "aiuola che ci fa tanto feroci." Dante had,
with a heavy heart, returned to the disappointing spectacle
of the low earthly world and then, with a determined turning
of his head, looked back to Beatrice, "poscia rivolsi gli occhi
agli occhi belli." Quite appropriately, with his customary,
exquisite sensitivity, Momigliano stressed the most important
element in the image of the bird that opens the canto, without, however, relating it to the remaining context: "Sicché
protagonista dell'immagine diventa, non l'uccello, ma il cielo
su cui il sole ha da sorgere." Indeed, he regarded the sky at
the moment of imminent daybreak as the "protagonist" of
the image, rather than the more obvious bird!

this description is one of the most impressive light effects in the poem:

> As under the sun's ray, which issueth pure through a broken cloud, ere now mine eyes have seen a meadow full of flowers, when themselves covered by the shade;
> so beheld I many a throng of splendors, glowed on from above by ardent rays, beholding not the source whence came the glowings.
>
> [Carlyle-Wicksteed trans.]

> (Come a raggio di sol che puro mei
>   per fratta nube già prato di fiori
>   vider, coverti d'ombra, li occhi miei;
> vid'io così più turbe di splendori,
>   fulgorate di su da raggi ardenti,
>   sanza veder principio di fulgori.)
>
> (ll. 79–84)

Beatrice, of course, the other woman, is ever-present, a participant in the triumph of femininity that fills the canto, all the closer to Dante in this next to last step into the open light and the full sun. It was indeed to Beatrice that the opening simile referred: as the mother-bird (a mother-bird, let us remember, opens the canto, just as the Virgin Mother closes it)[47] eagerly awaits the sun out of love for her little ones, so that she may see them and feed them (note the affectionate

47. St. Peter's "triumph" is an anticipation of episodes to come. Incidentally, Bosco's "lettura" cited above contains a page (16) of classical reminiscences, all of which referred to this initial image of the canto, in which Bosco also stresses the femininity and motherliness of the bird.

insistence on this explicit motivation, "amate fronde," "dolci nati," "li aspetti disiati," "gravi labor li sono aggrati," "ardente affetto"), so Beatrice awaits the coming of Christ, who will bring mystic food to Dante, her ward. Her face shows fullness of ardor ("paríemi che 'l suo viso ardesse tutto" [l. 22]), a clear parallel to the bird's ardente affetto.

We have, then, witnessed a shining example of broad, lyrical, "intuitive" texture rather than close logical context, and particularly of an image that is more a consequence of the "spirit" or state of mind of the canto than of the logic of the immediate comparison.[48] This functionality of the symbols within the aesthetic context should also warn us against the dangers inherent in going after the recurrent symbols as if they established a consistent rational pattern—a pattern important to discover in order to reveal the inner intellectual message of the poem, its moral and political cryptographic structure. Here, for instance, Mary is called a "rosa mistica," whereas a mystic rose in the Empyrean no longer stands for Mary. Likewise,

48. Lack of "logic" is not so uncommon in Dante. We have a telling example in this same canto, ll. 112–17, where the poet claims that the inner surface of the higher heaven, the "primum mobile," was made invisible to him by distance —an "unscientific" statement by the standards of his own metaphysical optics, but justified by the necessities of poetic representation—which, at that point, demanded the disappearance of Mary. (From the same Eighth Heaven he had been able to see, in the other direction, all the way down to the earth, and to see the "aiuola . . . tutta . . . da' colli alle foci.") We are reminded of the topographically conflicting sizes of "bolge" in Hell, the "miglia ventidue" immediately followed by "undici miglia" (*Inferno,* XXIX, 9, and XXX, 86), where Dante's basic indifference to actual measurements was evident.

the "ingigliarsi all'emme" in the transition to the Eagle of Jupiter has been regarded by some as a reference to Mary, whereas the lily here stands for the Apostles, not for Mary. The mode of being of Dante's imagery owes more to expressive needs than to the abstract intellectual structures of the poem, and this consideration should make the analyst of cryptographs cautious. If our analysis has succeeded in showing a case of this basic poetic truth, it will have attained its goal.

Index

INDEX

Esposito, E., 166 n.
Ezra, Ibn, 154 n.

Ficino, M., 151
Fitzgerald, Thomas A., 141 n., 159
Fogazzaro, A., 166 n.
Foster, K., 40 n.
Franciosi, G., 140 n.
Francis, St., 41, 51–53
Freud, Sigmund, 69
Frugoni, A., 30 n.
Fubini, M., 144 n., 146 n.

Gallo, Salvatore, 167 n.
Garin, E., 154 n.
Getto, Giovanni, 55 n., 152 n.
Gioachino da Fiore, 20, 40–42
Gmelin, Hermann, 167 n.
Grabher, Carlo, 144 n., 145 n.

Hegel, G. W. F., 116–18
Hopkins, G. M., 136

Imola, Benvenuto da, 138–39

Ker, W. P., 150 n.

Latham, Charles Sterrett, 54 n.
Latini, Brunetto, 27–28, 113–14
Lindner, Ernst, 156 n.
Lo Nigro, Sebastiano, 166 n.
Lotario, Giovanni, 41
Luiso, F. P., 36 n.

Macaulay, T. B., 158 n., 159, 163
McKeon, R., 139 n.
Maggini, F., 137 n., 140 n.
Malagoli, L., 156 n., 157 n.
Malispini, Ricordano, 34–36
Mark the Lombard, 22
Mazzeo, J. A., 152 n.
Migliorini, B., 156 n.
Milton, John, 158
Momigliano, Attilio, 153 n., 169 n.
Monarchia, 8, 53
Montano, R., 161 n., 166 n.
Monte, A. del, 34 n.
More, St. Thomas, 18
Morghen, Raffaello, 20 n., 21 n.

Nabholz, Hans, 34 n.
Nardi, Brunetto, 27 n., 51

Oddone di Cluny, 21
Olivero, F., 140 n., 160

Pagliaro, A., 141
Paul, St., 58
Pellegrini, F., 144 n., 166 n.
Peter of Albano, 154 n.
Petrarch, 6, 36
Plato, 75
Plotinus, 75–76
Poliziano, A., 151 n.
Porena, M., 144 n., 149 n., 162 n., 163 n., 165 n.
Pound, Ezra, 160 n.
Praz, M., 159 n.
Proclus, 76

Quintilian, 153

174

INDEX